Paths to Learning:
Teaching for Engagement in College

Barbara F. Tobolowsky, Editor

The National Resource Center for
The First-Year Experience® and Students in Transition
University of South Carolina

Cite as:
Tobolowsky, B. F. (Ed.). (2014). *Paths to learning: Teaching for engagement in college.* Columbia, SC: University of South Carolina, National Resource Center for The First-Year Experience and Students in Transition.

ISBN: 978-1-889-27192-7
Published by:
National Resource Center for
The First-Year Experience and Students in Transition
University of South Carolina
1728 College Street, Columbia, SC 29208
www.sc.edu/fye

Production Staff for the National Resource Center:

Project Manager:	Toni Vakos, Editor
Cover Design:	Josh Tyler, Graphic Artist
Composition and Layout:	Erin Morris, Graphic Designer
External Reviewers:	Brad Garner, Director of Faculty Enrichment and The Learning Academy Center for Learning and Innovation, Indiana Wesleyan University

Library of Congress Cataloging-in-Publication Data

Paths to learning : teaching for engagement in college / Barbara F. Tobolowsky, editor.
pages cm
Includes index.
ISBN 978-1-889271-92-7
1. College teaching. 2. Reflective learning. I. Tobolowsky, Barbara F., editor of compilation.
LB2331.P363 2014
378.1'25--dc23
2014011024

About the Publisher

The National Resource Center for The First-Year Experience and Students in Transition was born out of the success of University of South Carolina's much-honored University 101 course and a series of annual conferences on the freshman-year experience. The momentum created by the educators attending these early conferences paved the way for the development of the National Resource Center, which was established at the University of South Carolina in 1986. As the National Resource Center broadened its focus to include other significant student transitions in higher education, it underwent several name changes, adopting the National Resource Center for The First-Year Experience and Students in Transition in 1998.

Today, the Center collaborates with its institutional partner, University 101 Programs, in pursuit of its mission to advance and support efforts to improve student learning and transitions into and through higher education. We achieve this mission by providing opportunities for the exchange of practical and scholarly information as well as the discussion of trends and issues in our field through convening conferences and other professional development events, such as institutes, workshops, and online learning opportunities; publishing scholarly practice books, research reports, a peer-reviewed journal, electronic newsletters, and guides; generating, supporting, and disseminating research and scholarship; hosting visiting scholars; and maintaining several online channels for resource sharing and communication, including a dynamic website, listservs, and social media outlets. The National Resource Center serves as the trusted expert, internationally recognized leader, and clearinghouse for scholarship, policy, and best practice for all postsecondary student transitions.

Institutional Home

The National Resource Center is located at the University of South Carolina's (USC) flagship campus in Columbia. Chartered in 1801, USC Columbia's mission is twofold: (a) to establish and maintain excellence in its student population, faculty, academic programs, living and learning environment, technological infrastructure, library resources, research and scholarship, and public and private support and endowment; and (b) to enhance the industrial, economic, and cultural potential of the state. The Columbia campus offers 324 degree programs through its 14 degree-granting colleges and schools. Students have been awarded more than $16.7 million for national scholarships and fellowships since 1994. In fiscal year 2013, faculty generated $220 million in funding for research, outreach, and training programs. Carolina is one of only 63 public universities listed by the Carnegie Foundation in the highest tier of research institutions in the United States.

Contents

List of Figures

Foreword

As anyone who has stood in front of an auditorium of hundreds, taught a classroom or led a training of dozens, presided over a seminar of less than 20, or even mediated a conflict between two or three students can attest, facilitating the learning process is about much more than conveying content. It is about creating trust, examining existing knowledge with a critical eye, creating a safe space for questioning, and illustrating the relevance of knowledge. It is also the ability to help students use the fullest range of their cognitive processes to interact with information in increasingly complex ways, ultimately using their mastery of content to advance the discourse on a topic.

When framed in this fashion, it is no wonder that teachers are often overwhelmed by the task at hand. Any of us who have adopted the title of teacher, either temporarily or as our primary professional role, understand the myriad challenges embedded in the journey of facilitating students' learning. We are often looking for ideas, guidance, and tools to help us navigate the pathways to learning for our students and for ourselves. Yet, finding an appropriate, accessible, and, perhaps most importantly, efficient resource to assist us can be a challenge. Thus, despite the best of intentions and high level of commitment to our students, teachers often remain entrenched in outdated practices and engage less-than-optimal strategies.

The National Resource Center for The First-Year Experience and Students in Transition is pleased to offer this book to fill this void. As noted by the editor, Barbara Tobolowsky, and supported by the contributions of the chapter authors, this volume is intended to summarize the large body of research and theory on teaching and learning. It seeks to highlight a range of pedagogical approaches that show the most promise for today's diverse group of college learners, providing a road map to assist teachers and students in their journey down the paths of learning.

While this goal is, in and of itself, an important and meaningful accomplishment, I am especially pleased that the editor and authors produced a publication that demonstrates several of the core commitments of the National Resource Center in its content. For example, the book is dedicated to the process of lifelong learning, most notably with respect to learning *about* learning. As educators, we are committed to what the Center identifies in its mission statement as an "ongoing process of inquiry, exploration, and discovery," even in our work to examine how we initiate and nurture these processes in our students.

This book also firmly situates itself within the scholarship of practice and highlights the connection between research and practice. It pays homage to the history of learning theories that have emerged from previous scholarship and provides an overview of recent research on engaged learning to situate the discussion of various pedagogical approaches. In turn, these approaches are informed by scholarship and represent current thinking in an ongoing research agenda on teaching and learning. By positioning this work in the liminal space between research and practice, the volume advances both scholarly practice and applied research on pedagogy and learning.

We also hope it is evident to the reader that this book is deeply embedded in an ethos of inclusion. It seeks to address the academic needs and cognitive development of a diverse student body with respect to age, race/ethnicity, socioeconomic status, family status, academic preparation, employment, and affiliation with a host of student identities that may represent historically underrepresented or at-risk groups, such as adult learners, returning students, transfers, first-generation, and veterans. The teaching practices featured in this volume are intended to reach the widest range of students by incorporating a variety of different learning approaches; vehicles for intellectual exploration; delivery methods; and teaching platforms, such as in-person, online, and hybrid approaches. Together, these ideas and commitment to inclusion advance a social justice imperative as part of student development, learning, and success.

Finally, the content of these chapters represents a collaborative approach to learning. Connections are drawn between the students themselves in several examples of peer engagement in the classroom and interactive or cooperative learning strategies. However, one of the goals of this book is to also challenge the historic assumption and practice of hierarchy in the classroom with the teacher as the purveyor of knowledge and the students as the recipients. Instead, the chapter authors highlight classroom techniques that engage the strengths of both students *and* the teacher(s) in the learning process and allow for a coconstruction of the learning space, process, and outcomes. Collaboration between learner and teacher is pivotal to the process of intellectual exploration and expansion. The fact that this book represents a partnership between researchers and academics from various institutional environments and professional backgrounds further illustrates the dedication to the value of collaboration.

This book lived as a dream long before it came to fruition and is the result of many people's dedication and efforts to see these ideas documented on the pages herein. I would like to thank the editor, Barbara Tobolowsky, the extremely talented group of chapter authors, and the publications staff of the National Resource Center for lending their time, experience, analysis, and expertise to this project. We are pleased to add this volume to the Center's library of scholarly practice books and hope it will serve as a valuable resource for practice, a foundation for future research, and an inspiration for teachers everywhere to enhance the classroom experiences of their students and clear their paths to learning.

Jennifer R. Keup
Director
National Resource Center for
The First-Year Experience and Students in Transition
University of South Carolina

Chapter 1
Paths to Learning: An Introduction

Barbara F. Tobolowsky

In 2002, I joined the staff of the National Resource Center for The First-Year Experience and Students in Transition as its third associate director. Around that time, John Gardner, our former director, spoke with Darlene Hantzis about writing a monograph for the Center on feminist pedagogies and the first year of college. Darlene was unavailable then, so Tracy Skipper and I added the idea to our list of potential future monographs, which we revisited over the years. As things turned out, the timing was never right for one reason or another, but we remained committed to writing the book one day. When I left the Center in 2009, Tracy, Toni (now on staff at the Center), and I agreed that if this volume materialized, I would be involved in some way. In 2012, I finally got the call.

We realized there were a number of issues in higher education that made it an ideal time to move the book idea from the back to front burner. The first of those concerns came in 2011 from the bombshell book, *Academically Adrift* (Arum & Roksa, 2011). The powerful sound bite from the book was that students were not learning to the desired degree during the college years. Arum and Roksa's (2011) results inflamed the public, policymakers, and educators from coast to coast.

Although some researchers (e.g., Astin, 2011) have questioned the methodological approach and findings since the book's publication, nothing seemed to defuse what felt like a broadside attack on higher education, in general, and faculty, who were singled out as part of the problem, in particular. Perhaps the reason the book's claim hit so hard was because it questioned the very purpose of a postsecondary education at a time when the cost of college was also being challenged. How could institutions of higher education justify their price tag if students were not developing their critical-thinking, reasoning, and writing skills during college?

A second tension that prompted the book is related to the general nature of this and other critiques. Most of them assume a monolithic view of higher education, which does not accurately represent the nature of higher education today. From public to private, small to large, research to liberal arts to community college, and online to brick and mortar, higher education institutions are more diverse than ever before. Different types of schools have different missions (Morphew & Hartley, 2006) that lead to different outcomes. However, this variability is lost in these broad-brush criticisms that seem to suggest that all institutions are the same.

Often, a generalized view of institutions leads to a generalized view of students, which is also inaccurate. For instance, college rankings from *U.S. News & World Report,* which is the most likely way the public gets institutional information (Redden, 2013), focus on the experience of traditional students (i.e., first-time, full-time, residing on campus, traditional aged), assuming all students fit this profile. However, only 15% of students today are considered to be traditional (Hess, 2011). Therefore, this small segment of the student population is determining the reputation of an institution.

So who are our students? Nontraditional students have become the majority on many campuses. These students tend to be older, having delayed enrollment because of financial (Advisory Committee, 2012) or other personal reasons. They may also be students of color, financially independent from their parents, the first in their family to attend college, full-time workers, single parents, attending college part-time, and/or coming from a low socio-economic class (Horn & Carroll, 1996). In addition, they are more likely not to follow a straight progression through college (i.e., graduating from the same institution they initially enrolled in) since more than half of today's students attend more than one institution during their college experience (Adelman, 2006).

And, that experience varies greatly depending on the student's circumstances. For instance, a 35-year-old student who works full-time and attends a community college after first going to a four-year institution (a reverse transfer) experiences and expects different things from the college experience than a 19-year-old enrolled at a residential college. What this means for faculty is they need to serve a wide variety of students at a diverse set of institutions with different available resources. This rebuttal is not meant to ignore the fact there may be issues at certain types of institutions or for some students, only that it is important to be specific about where there are problems and what those problems are and for whom, so they can be addressed in a responsible and meaningful way (Bok, 2013).

In addition to these tensions, a third event affecting our classrooms is the shift to providing online educational options. Online education in some form plays a critical role in higher education today. Some states (e.g., Texas) are demanding a less expensive college degree, which relies on the use of online courses and/or programs. The reasons are clear. Institutions gain additional revenue and improve their graduation rates (if successful), and students appreciate the flexibility of these offerings (Jos Vias, 2008). As a result, online enrollments are on the rise. In 2009, there was a 4% increase (from 17% to 21%) in the number of students enrolled in online courses with a total of 5.6 million taking at least one online course (Kaya, 2010). This increase is seen at all types of institutions. In fact, "more public colleges than private non-profits—74.9 percent versus 60.5 percent—say it's [online education] part of their long-term plans" (Kaya, 2010, para. 3). Consequently, blended (online and in-class elements) and all-online courses have changed the educational landscape.

A more recent technological phenomenon is the arrival of the massive online open courses (MOOCs). These free, large courses have provoked a lot of attention since their initial introduction in the summer of 2011, with many institutions rushing to jump on the MOOC bandwagon. However, today some institutions (e.g., Amherst College, American University) have put the brakes on, wanting to determine if this offering makes sense for their students (Kolowich, 2013). Other institutions have taken the concept of MOOCs in a new direction. In the fall of 2013, 16 colleges and universities offered a DOCC, or distributed open collaborative course, which takes some of the technological elements of MOOCs but uses them to support brick-and-mortar classroom discussions (Jaschik, 2013). In these instances, instructors from multiple institutions will use the same video featuring an expert in the field (like a MOOC) to introduce the week's theme. However, unlike MOOCs, this "technology enhanced learning environment" allows campus-based instructors to create a unique classroom experience by developing their own syllabus for their class of 15 to 30 undergraduate or graduate students, recognizing that students have valuable knowledge and expertise to share in a traditional classroom setting (Juhasz as cited in Jaschik, 2013, para. 14).

The fact that not all institutions are choosing to ride these current trends may reflect caution, thoughtfulness, or resistance to change. And, at this point, it is anyone's guess how much or little MOOCs, DOCCs, or other innovations will change higher education. Yet, regardless of the ultimate direction higher education takes, all of these events and formats bring new challenges to the professoriate, and a host of questions emerge: What is the job of the instructor? How do the current tensions affect how faculty teach? How do instructors address the needs of a diverse group of students? How do faculty adapt to the constantly changing terrain of higher education? Nevertheless, before we attempt to address some of these questions with this book, it may be helpful to briefly discuss the history of pedagogical practice that led us to the current situation.

A Historical View

Any historical discussion about education begins with the Greeks. Both Plato and Socrates are well known for their educational views. In *The Republic*, Plato (360 BCE/1974), Socrates's student, explained that education was important because it led to the health and success of the city-state. The educational goal was goodness of character. Exposure to the arts and humanities was critical to him because it was through this exposure learners were able to discern what makes a virtuous character.

In addition to these philosophical views, the beginnings of many pedagogic practices used today are seen in these early examples as well. For instance, pedagogically, debate and discussion were at the heart of Plato and Socrates's approaches to teaching, since these methods bring to light contradictions and a deeper understanding of the truth. Another specific tool Socrates introduced was a version of peer feedback. He used inner and outer circles of students to discuss topics of interest—the inner circle discussed (or debated) a passage of text, while the outer circle observed and took notes during the discussion. When the discussion was over, the students in the outer circle provided feedback to those engaged in the debate. Students alternated roles in future discussions. This way all students got the opportunity to discuss and critique over time.

In 1762, Jean-Jacques Rousseau (1762/1979) published *Emile* (also known as *On Education*) to present his views on education. In the book, he advocated learning through exploration. He explained, "let them [students] learn nothing in books which experience can teach them" (p. 251). Further, he felt it was important to teach at the students' level and not above, so they would maintain their curiosity and interest. His hands-on approach to differentiated learning was echoed hundreds of years later in John Dewey's work.

Dewey (1938) felt the teacher's role was to facilitate the student's experience. Like a successful chess player, the teacher must consider what is already known about a topic and the unique characteristics of that student to help guide her or him into various experiences to stimulate learning. The basic elements of this approach are to focus on learning through experience rather than through textbooks. For example, instead of talking about principles in the abstract, Dewey advocated grounding the learning in everyday experiences to which the student could relate. This approach would inspire ongoing curiosity and, in turn, the desire to learn. Dewey was opposed to the instructor who "ladle[s] out [what is known] in doses" (p. 381). Therefore, he did not believe the teacher was the repository of all knowledge controlling what, when, and how students gained information. Learning was an active event, which faculty facilitated.

Similarly, Lev Vygotsky (1926/1997) believed the role of the teacher was to support learning by teaching students how to "acquire such knowledge and to make use of it" (p. 339). Over time, that level of support would lessen until the students were able to work independently. Vygotsky described this changing role of students when he said,

> Until now the student has always stood on the teachers' shoulders. He has looked upon everything through the teacher's eyes and judged everything by the way his teacher thought. The time has come to place the student on his own two feet and to recognize that there is not very much knowledge the teacher can impart to the student. ... The child must himself be made to walk and to fall, to suffer pain from injuries, and to decide what direction to follow. (p. 342)

This view recognizes the value of students playing an active role in their learning and experiencing failures. It is only through these experiences that students learn. Further, Vygotsky is credited with the concept of scaffolding—guiding students through the process of getting and using information on their own. In practice, this could be done through a class exercise that uses a concept and then has students complete a similar exercise on their own. In this way, students gain the skills and confidence by doing the lesson in class, which they then use in a different context later. This results in students becoming active, independent learners.

In spite of the fact that many educators from the earliest days have advocated a more engaging approach to pedagogy, one might wonder where the lecture approach came from and why it has had such an enduring hold on the professoriate. Cohen and Kisker (2010) detailed the history of higher education instruction and explained the varying reasons lecture started and stayed a primary teaching method since the founding of colonial colleges. The main reasons for its dominance seemed to be practical. At the first colleges, books were not readily available, so faculty needed to provide the information. And, because education was about developing taste and not adding to the knowledge base, as it was in the time of the Greeks, students focused on memorizing and reciting what was known and recognized as "truth" (Cohen & Kisker, 2010).

Since those early days, there have been many curricular developments, such as the addition of electives and the development of disciplines, which have led to faculty specialization and a shift from content acquisition to making new discoveries (Cohen & Kisker, 2010). By the late 1880s, faculty were balancing teaching with research at many institutions. This division between liberal arts and research created a tension regarding the purpose of higher education. Where Harvard University and the University of Virginia represented the research agenda, Yale faculty fought for the more traditional, classical approach (Rudolph, 1990). In fact, they famously supported the importance of a traditional curriculum that focused on offering a liberal education in the *Yale Report of 1828*, which other institutions used to support a similar goal (Cohen & Kisker, 2010). This division reflects one of the first signs of institutional diversity that was beginning to take root in the United States. There was no longer one type of institution serving a select population of students.

Other institutional, legislative, and social changes led to additional transformations in the academy. For example, the first Morrill Act in 1862 established land-grant colleges, which brought students to the academy who were interested in engineering and agriculture. Almost 40 years later, junior colleges (now known as community colleges) were established to provide remedial and vocational education (Cohen & Brawer, 2008). With institutional diversity, student populations continued to grow more diverse as well. This shift reflected the belief that a postsecondary education was no longer the province of only the elite but for everyone who wanted one. This belief was solidified with the passage of the GI Bill in 1944 that supported the influx of military veterans into the higher education system.

Societal events also affected the academy (Cohen & Kisker, 2010). The civil rights movement, the war in Vietnam, and the space race were just some events that had an impact on the curriculum, which, in turn, changed the professoriate. For example, the feminist movement in the 1970s and 1980s paralleled scholarly work (e.g., Gilligan, 1982; Josselson, 1978) that explored different ways women approached knowledge and learning. As the scholarship expanded, notions of pedagogy did as well. To explain, a critical component of the feminist movement was the notion of consciousness raising, which was a process where small groups of women met to discuss, share, and "come to better understand ... their lives" (Boxer, 1998, p. 20). Insights from this practice contributed to pedagogical shifts from lecture to discussion and the teacher as facilitator rather than the expert. The increase of females in the professoriate also supported these shifts. In addition, these changes fit well with the work of Paolo Freire and other critical theorists (see Chapter 4) who came to similar conclusions by different routes around the same time. As a result, more quantitative approaches (e.g., lecture) in the classroom made way for more qualitative ones, such as discussion (Stromquist, 1999).

In spite of these developments, the most common teaching method remained the lecture. Efficiency in the classroom has always been an important motivator in higher education (Cohen & Kisker, 2010). For some, lecture ensures students are given information that can then be easily assessed with objective tests (e.g., multiple choice questions on computer-scored forms). Subjective methods of testing (e.g., papers and essays) are more challenging and time consuming for the instructor to grade and may not measure content acquisition as easily. Nevertheless, as the conversation shifted from teaching to learning, the central question was, Which methods lead to learning that lasts? Researchers found it was the pedagogies that used active-learning techniques that led to increased learning (McCarthy & Anderson, 2000).

Evidence of the value of these more innovative approaches was supported by the work of Astin (1991), who advocated talent development, a concept suggesting that college is supposed to add value rather than have students hit some arbitrary standard of knowledge. A decade later, Kuh and colleagues (2005) found through Project DEEP (Documenting Effective Educational Practice) that more engaging pedagogies produced greater learning. This supported the development of new assessment tools, such as the National Survey of Student Engagement (NSSE) and the Collegiate Learning Assessment (CLA), that look beyond mere knowledge acquisition to the use of engaging pedagogies and their link to student learning.

The Purpose of This Book

Today, higher education is again in the crosshairs of multiple tensions as stated above. Still, at its core, it is an enterprise devoted to student learning. Teachers who are dedicated to this goal may feel at a loss regarding ways to more fully engage their diverse students. As a faculty member myself, I struggle with facilitating my students' learning, adopting constantly changing technological tools, and attempting to provide differentiated instruction that helps students wherever they are. Over the years, I picked up various books for help; and although I learned from all of them, the deep, but narrow focus of these resources frustrated me. With limited time, I looked for a "best of" book that would offer an overview of a range of theoretically based approaches to give me ideas on what may work best for my students and for me. I found no such work in the marketplace. It is from this brew of events and challenges that the idea of the book took its final shape.

You will notice two main changes from that original idea discussed by John Gardner and Darlene Hantzis. First, the volume is not focused on the first year. Student challenges do not end in the first year, so these chapters speak more generally to the undergraduate experience. Second, although the book's initial focus was on feminist pedagogy, now it has expanded to cover a range of theoretical approaches that seem to be of particular interest today.

The book begins with two foundational chapters to provide a context for the other chapters. Jillian Kinzie in Chapter 2 summarizes the most current research on the important role engagement plays in learning. Then James Groccia and his colleagues give an overview of some key theoretical approaches to teaching and learning in Chapter 3. They discuss six different theoretical families from behaviorism to andragogy. Although there are distinctions between pedagogy (teaching children) and andragogy (teaching adults), I should note you will find a more generalized use of the term *pedagogy* in most chapters. For the purposes of this book, it will serve as the term for teaching all students, even adults.

In Chapter 4, Nana Osei-Kofi returns to that original kernel of the idea for the book by discussing critical pedagogy more broadly. Although not strictly a pedagogical method, there are ways to incorporate elements of this theory within the classroom. The next three chapters look at more specific pedagogical approaches. Laura Rendón and Vijay Kanagala write about contemplative pedagogy in Chapter 5, which involves engaging students in learning through introspection and other meditative practices. Then, in Chapter 6, Laurie Schreiner describes strengths-based pedagogy and how valuing students' contributions can produce greater learning. James Groccia and his colleagues, in Chapter 7, introduce integrative group learning methods and then give examples that include collaborative, cooperative, and problem-based learning strategies.

Chapters 8 and 9 capture the current thinking about two topics of particular interest today: (a) online or blended classes and (b) assessment. Amy Collier has the task of covering the issue of engagement in online or blended classrooms, providing information about both the current status and use of technological tools, while Wendy Troxel tackles the topic of classroom assessment. Over the years, I have often heard colleagues express interest in attempting new approaches to teaching only to feel stymied by how to grade these efforts. Unable to overcome their assessment challenges, they end up making only marginal changes to a course rather than rethinking their approach. In Chapter 9, Wendy helps to break down the large topic of classroom assessment in a way that makes it applicable regardless of the specific pedagogical choice. Finally, in the last chapter, I offer a summary of the key findings from the volume to help readers as they consider adapting and adopting some of these practices in their own classrooms.

This book is an attempt to provide a succinct view of some pedagogical paths available to faculty. Each chapter is grounded in theory while offering examples of how these theories can be applied in a classroom. We hope it offers you the sort of "best of" overview that results in sharpening your skills and, in turn, helping your students become more confident learners who will prosper now and in the future.

References

Adelman, C. (2006). *The toolbox revisited: Paths to degree completion from high school through college.* Washington, DC: U.S. Department of Education.

Advisory Committee on Student Financial Assistance (2012, February). *Pathways to success: Integrating learning with life and work to increase national college completion.* Retrieved from www2ed.gov/about/bdscomm/list/acsfa/ptsreport2.pdf

Arum, R., & Roksa, J. (2011). *Academically adrift: Limited learning on college campuses.* Chicago, IL: University of Chicago Press.

Astin, A. W. (1991). *Achieving educational excellence.* San Francisco, CA: Jossey-Bass.

Astin, A. W. (2011, February 14). In 'Academically Adrift,' data don't back up sweeping claim. *The Chronicle of Higher Education.* Retrieved from http://chronicle.com/article/Academically-Adrift-a/126371/

Bok, D. (2013). *Higher education in America.* Princeton, NJ: Princeton University Press.

Boxer, M. J. (1998). *When women ask the questions: Creating women's studies in America.* Baltimore, MD: The Johns Hopkins University Press.

Cohen, A. M., & Brawer, F. B. (2008). *The American community college* (5th ed.). San Francisco, CA: Jossey-Bass.

Cohen, A. M., & Kisker, C. B. (2010). *The shaping of American higher education: Emergence and growth of the contemporary system* (2nd ed.). San Francisco, CA: Jossey-Bass.

Dewey, J. (1938). *Experience and education* (Kappa Delta Pi lecture series). New York, NY: Macmillian.

Gilligan, C. (1982). *In a different voice: Psychological theory and women's development.* Cambridge, MA: Harvard University Press.

Hess, F. (2011, September 28). Old school: College's most important trend is the rise of the adult student. *The Atlantic.* Retrieved from www.theatlantic.com/business/archive/2011/09/old-school-colleges-most-important-trend-is-the-rise-of-the-adult-student/245823/

Horn, L. J., & Carroll, C. D. (1996). *Nontraditional undergraduates: Trends in enrollment from 1986 to 1992 and persistence and attainment among 1989-90 beginning postsecondary students.* Washington, DC: National Center for Education Statistics.

Jaschik, S. (2013, Aug. 19). Feminist professors create an alternative to MOOCs. *Inside Higher Education.* Retrieved from http://www.insidehighered.com/news/2013/08/19/feminist-professors-create-alternative-moocs

Jos Vias, M. (2008, Oct. 10). Why a small liberal-arts college decided to offer online courses. *The Chronicle of Higher Education.* Retrieved from chronicle.com/article/Why-a-Small-Liberal-Arts/22080/

Josselson, R. (1978). *Finding herself: Pathways to identity development of women.* San Francisco, CA: Jossey-Bass.

Kaya, T. (2010, Nov. 16). Enrollment in online courses increases at the highest rate ever. *Chronicle of Higher Education.* Retrieved from http://chronicle.com/blogs/wiredcampus/enrollment-in-online-courses-increases-at-the-highest-rate-ever/28204

Kolowich, S. (2013, April 29). Why some colleges are saying no to MOOCS, at least for now. *The Chronicle of Higher Education.* Retrieved from http://chronicle.com/article/Why-Some-Colleges-are-saying/138863/

Kuh, G. D., Kinzie, J., Schuh, J. H., Whitt, E. J., & Associates (2005). *Student success college: Creating conditions that matter.* San Francisco, CA: Jossey-Bass.

McCarthy, J. P., & Anderson, L. (2000). Active learning techniques versus traditional teaching styles: Two experiments from history and political science. *Innovative Higher Education, 24*(4), 279-294.

Morphew, C. C., & Hartley, M. (2006). Mission statements: A thematic analysis of rhetoric across institutional type. *The Journal of Higher Education, 77*(3), 456-471.

Plato (1974). *Plato's republic* (G.M.A. Grube, Trans.). Indianapolis, IN: Hackett Publishing Co. (Original work published 360 BCE)

Redden, E. (2013, July 25). Different kind of ranking? *Inside Higher Education.* Retrieved from www.insidehighered.com/news/2013/o7/25/controversial-u-multirank-initiative-aspires-be-different-kind-international-ranking#.UhZaS7wpf9h

Rousseau, J. J. (1979). *Emile, on education* (A. Bloom, Trans.). New York, NY: Basic Books. (Original work published 1762)

Rudolph, F. (1990). *The American college and university: A history.* Athens, GA: University of Georgia Press.

Stromquist, N. P. (1999). The global emergence of a field: Content, form, and promise in women's studies. In J. C. Smart (Ed.), *Higher education: Handbook of theory and research* (pp. 437-467). Bronx, NY: Agathon Press.

Vygotsky, L. S. (1997). *Educational psychology* (R. Silverman, Trans.). Boca Rotan, FL: St Lucie Press. (Original work published 1926)

Yale College. (1828). *Reports on the course of instruction in Yale College by a committee of the corporation, and the academical faculty.* Retrieved from http://www.yale.edu/terc/collectiblesandpublications/specialdocuments/Historical_Documents/1828_curriculum.pdf

Chapter 2
Research on Successful Learning Practices

Jillian Kinzie

Today's higher education institutions are confronted by current critiques regarding how much students learn and skepticism about the value of undergraduate education. Yet, while there is explicit pressure for postsecondary education to demonstrably improve the quality of learning and student success, the strategy for making these improvements is not always clear cut. One approach to addressing current pressures is to focus more explicitly on student learning and, in particular, use research-based approaches to inform improvements in undergraduate education. This strategy requires greater awareness of research on student learning and a willingness to change the conditions for learning on campus.

Fortunately, it seems that college educators are more interested in the learning processes of their students than ever before (Doyle, 2008). These perspective shifts underscore the need to understand what matters to learning. What are optimal experiences and settings for learning? What instructional practices are most likely to produce learning for more students? What aspects of the total college environment enhance students' learning?

The design of effective undergraduate education demands greater understanding and use of research-based approaches. This chapter introduces foundational concepts and research on practices that lead to learning, beginning with the particulars of effective education practice followed by an overview of the literature on engaging pedagogy and instructional practice.

Overview of Research on Learning

Research about learning in college draws from a wide base and several disciplines, including psychology; philosophy; sociology; and more recently, neuroscience. Learning in college is a complex process, which is influenced by intellectual, social, and emotional characteristics as well as the development of the learner, the conditions and structures of the learning environment, the quality of teaching, and the integration of all of these factors. Learning theories attempt to explain various types of learning, including (a) behavioral theories, which emphasize the forming of associations between stimuli and responses through selective reinforcement, and (b) cognitive theories that explain learning in terms of information processing and student perceptions of peers, teachers, and materials. (See Chapter 3 for more on foundational learning theories.) Effective learning environments require the specification of relevant theoretical perspectives for the types of learning in the college context and draw on these perspectives to design learning practice.

Learning theories are usually tied closely to educational practices, and teaching and learning are often inseparably linked. However, these connections are all too frequently ignored in practice. In fact, educational practices employed in college tend to be based more on modeling, trial and error, or intuitive guesswork than on theories of learning or research on effective learning practices.

A considerable body of research reveals a lot about learning in college and the general practices that promote college student learning. Pascarella and Terenzini (2005) synthesized hundreds of studies on the impact of general instructional approaches. The research includes evidence of the impact of learning outside the classroom, class size, institution-wide climate to support learning, and general activities for learning. This vast body of research also explores specific strategies and their influence on learning, such as active and collaborative learning, supplemental instruction, first-year seminars, peer teaching, and structures such as learning communities in which groups of students are in a formal program taking two or more classes together. Several of these specific topics, including learning theories, critical pedagogy, and cooperative and collaborative learning, are explored in subsequent chapters in this volume. Therefore, this chapter focuses, more broadly, on research regarding specific learning strategies that contribute to student learning.

Framework of Effective Educational Practice

Current pressures to improve student learning are driving attention to evidence-based practices. Correspondingly, since issuing their first volume on this topic in 1991, Pascarella and Terenzini (2005) noted the expansion of research on the effect of college on student learning and a broader vision of how students learn. The expansion is related in part to more research on the increasingly diverse, national undergraduate student body and the need to understand what accounts for variations in outcomes by factors including age, race/ethnicity, gender, full- and part-time status, and institutional type. This view of how students learn went beyond a simple perspective that described learning as an act of acquiring facts and concepts marked by achievement of verifiable outcomes, to a view of students actively constructing and creating knowledge by making sense of the content and their experiences. This perspective has led to a range of innovative instructional approaches (e.g., collaborative and cooperative learning, problem-based learning, service-learning), which is the basis for this examination of research on successful learning practices.

The research discussed in the next section explores recent developments in neuroscience and how it informs teaching and learning, followed by the particulars of effective education practice. Specifically, the section looks at educational interventions proven to contribute to college student learning.

Research on Neuroscience

Some theories of learning are explained by differences in styles and traits. Learning styles are typically included in discussions about promoting students' learning. Although learning differences are more often the result of preferences or experiences rather than some inborn trait of the individual, they can be useful to introduce students to a wider range of strategies to help them master material in a meaningful way. Introducing students to their preferences in order to build a wider repertoire of study strategies can help them engender new ways to study and prepare for class.

More recently, neuroscience, cognitive science, or the study of the brain, has provided new fundamental insights into the many processes that influence learning. The work of Bransford, Brown, and Cocking (2000) offers a comprehensive overview of the field of neuroscience, exploring how to link the findings of research on the science of learning to the practice of teaching and learning. Recommendations to create learning-centered environments that pay careful attention to the knowledge, skills, attitudes, and beliefs that learners bring to the educational setting are vital.

This approach has been labeled *culturally responsive* and *culturally relevant* (Ladson-Billings, 1995), and attempts to draw out what students understand in relation to the problems on hand, discuss their misconceptions sensitively, and create new learning situations that allow for a readjustment of their ideas.

Work in neuroscience has reinforced learning theory research. For example, as in cognitive and constructivist theories of learning, a key finding in the science of learning is the importance of feedback and assessment. Opportunities for feedback, such as online monitoring of both group work and individual performance, can be formal and informal and should occur continuously as a part of instruction. Effective teachers also help students build skills of self-assessment—an important part of the metacognitive approach to instruction. However, because metacognition takes the form of an internal dialogue, requiring students to monitor their own understanding, many students may be unaware of its importance unless the processes are explicitly emphasized by instructors (Pintrich, 2002)—and contextualized by discipline. Bransford et al. (2000) suggested that in history, for example, students must think about who authored the reading and how this may affect the interpretation of events; whereas, in physics, students are monitoring their understanding of the underlying physical principle at work. As students learn to assess their own understandings and work, as well as the work of their peers, everyone learns more effectively.

Although some fear brain science research is too new and untested to apply in educational settings, Sousa's (2011) recent work includes new information about how the brain can affect teaching and learning. These findings show how sleep deprivation and stress influence learning; explore the effect of emotions on learning, memory, and recall; and challenge the notion that the brain can multitask.

Brain research fundamentally asserts the following conclusions about learning: (a) practice increases learning, (b) environment makes a difference, (c) learning changes the physical structures of the brain, (d) learning organizes and reorganizes the brain, and (e) emotion is the glue that holds learning together (Zull, 2002). Brain research also suggests the most important lesson for teaching is the role of prior learning. In particular, what learners bring to the learning environment—their beliefs, cultural backgrounds, knowledge of academic content, and study strategies—determines the ease or difficulty of their learning. Learners use current knowledge to construct new knowledge, and what they know and believe at the moment affects how they interpret new information. This suggests that educators must take time to gather information about their students and use the teaching tools of analogy, metaphor, simile, and example to build concrete experiences with which students can connect.

This research can help inform choices about teaching strategies. Selecting techniques, such as inquiry-based learning, lecturing, or cooperative learning, should be based on what is important for students to experience at that point or how to achieve a particular learning goal. For example, hands-on and application experiences may be appropriate to ground emergent knowledge, lecturing might be a way to excite imagination, and small-group learning could be the most effective way to provide students feedback on their preconceptions and apply emerging understandings. Knowing more about how people learn allows instructors to purposefully diversify their repertoire and develop a rich set of opportunities to construct an educational program.

Effective Educational Practice Research

Coincident with national calls for improvement in undergraduate education beginning in the late 1980s, significant attention has been dedicated to asserting what contributes to quality undergraduate learning and delineating effective approaches to teaching and learning. For example, the Education Commission of the States (1995) outlined 12 attributes for delivering a quality undergraduate education, concluding that when colleges and universities systematically engage in these good practices, student performance and satisfaction improve.

These 12 attributes (Education Commission of the States, 1995) broadly identify aspects of an institution's organizational culture and values, its curriculum, and the type of instructional practice needed for effective undergraduate education (Figure 2.1). Undergraduate quality begins with a campus culture that (a) sets high expectations for student learning and makes active efforts to help students reach them; (b) designs curricula and instructional efforts to meet students' diverse backgrounds, levels of preparation, and previous experiences; and (c) emphasizes the first years of undergraduate study and the importance of transition and challenging core academic experiences. A quality undergraduate curriculum demands coherence in learning experiences and reinforcement of specific outcomes, multiple opportunities in and outside the classroom for synthesizing experiences, practice of learned skills, and integration and application. Quality undergraduate instruction builds on active learning that requires regular discussion, considerable written work, application and demonstration experiences, frequent feedback on performance, collaborative learning with peers, substantive contact with faculty, and adequate time-on-task. These practices are important individually and are mutually reinforcing, and continue to be asserted as a foundation for educational quality.

Quality begins with an organizational culture that values
- High expectations
- Respect for diverse talents and learning styles
- Emphasis on early years of study

Quality curriculum requires
- Coherence in learning
- Synthesizing experiences
- Ongoing practice of learned skills
- Integrating education and experience

Quality instruction builds in
- Active learning
- Assessment and prompt feedback
- Collaboration
- Out-of-class contact with faculty
- Adequate time-on-task

Figure 2.1. Attributes of quality undergraduate education. Source: *Making Quality Count in Undergraduate Education,* Education Commission of the States (1995).

More specific to teaching, summaries of research on effective educational practice have generally advocated for active and experiential learning. The *Seven Principles for Good Practice in Undergraduate Education,* developed by a group of scholars of higher education and derived from the past 50 years of research, outlined a set of standards to improve learning (Chickering & Gamson, 1987; 1991), including (a) engaging in student-faculty contact, (b) encouraging cooperation among students, (c) using active-learning techniques, (d) providing prompt and meaningful feedback, (e) emphasizing time-on-task, (f) communicating high expectations, and (g) respecting diverse talents and ways of learning. Although each of the seven principles can stand alone, when all are present, their effects multiply and can exert a powerful force in undergraduate education.

This short list of empirically based, common-sense principles has been influential in broadening approaches to pedagogy on college campuses. The practices have been associated with many desirable outcomes, hold meaning for learning across professional programs and the liberal arts, and foster learning among all students—including across racial/ethnic groups, ages, socioeconomic statuses, genders, and levels of preparation (Cruce, Wolniak, Seifert, & Pascarella, 2006;

Mayhew, Wolniak, & Pascarella, 2008; Pascarella, Salisbury, & Blaich, 2011; Pascarella & Terenzini, 2005). Further, the principles assert the responsibility of educators and college and university leaders to foster an environment favorable to good practice in higher education.

Delving Deeper Into Principles of Good Practice

Evidence of the value of the seven principles as good practice for undergraduate education is robust. The research base for the principles is briefly reviewed in this section as well as other good practice techniques and strategies.

Student-faculty interaction has been well documented to have a positive impact on academic, social, and personal growth and development. Research by Pascarella and Terenzini (1991, 2005) and Astin (1984), among others, delineates the role of faculty in promoting students' academic achievement, persistence in college, and other educational outcomes, including cognitive, intellectual, and academic self-concept and career choice measures (Berger & Milem, 2000; Delaney, 2008; Kuh & Hu, 2001; Lundberg & Schreiner, 2004; Pascarella & Blaich, 2013; Umbach & Wawrzynski, 2005). Informal student-faculty interaction activities—being a guest in a professor's home, working on a research project with a faculty member, talking with instructors outside of class, and serving on committees with faculty—are positively correlated with student learning and development (Astin, 1993b; Kuh, 2003; Kuh & Hu, 2001). In addition, intentional programs to facilitate student-faculty interaction have different effects on students. For example, relationships with faculty predicted development of academic competence among new students in the first year of college (Reason, Terenzini, & Domingo, 2006) and sophomore success, in terms of GPA and satisfaction (Graunke & Woosley, 2005; Juillerat, 2000). Further, student-faculty interaction is also important because it encourages students to devote greater effort to other educationally purposeful activities.

Cooperative learning techniques, often grouped together with active learning in discussions about teaching and learning research, are effective in helping students learn content, promoting increased investigation of the subject, and fostering greater diligence in learning course material. These strategies are particularly useful to new students because they are effective in building camaraderie and forming support networks in early college years (Koprowski & Perigo, 2000; Slavin, 1990; Zambreno, Hoover, Anderson, & Gillman, 2002). Cooperative, and more specifically, problem-based learning have also been found to enhance student learning (Slavin, 1990; Smith, Sheppard, Johnson, & Johnson, 2005). Of course, the practice of cooperative learning must be carefully constructed by the instructor, and students must understand and be held accountable for their responsibility to the group. Important disciplinary approaches and techniques for effective group learning have been tested and constructed. For example, Michaelsen, Knight, and Fink (2004) detailed approaches to *team-based learning*, a strategy that provides students the opportunity to practice using course concepts to solve problems. (See Chapter 7 for more on cooperative and collaborative learning.)

Active learning encompasses activities in which students engage in a classroom other than listening passively to an instructor's lecture. A large amount of research confirms the benefits of active learning for promoting content acquisition, course success and satisfaction, and persistence to the next term (Bonwell & Eison, 1991; Braxton, Jones, Hirschy, & Hartley, 2008; Faust & Paulson, 1998; Hake, 1998; McKeachie & Svinicki, 2006; Silberman, 1996). Active learning has also been shown to be effective in online learning environments (Durrington, Berryhill, & Swafford, 2006). (See Chapter 8 for more on online pedagogies.) Commonly used and proven active-learning techniques include the *one-minute-paper*, a short in-class writing activity on a posed question (Angelo & Cross, 1993); reading quizzes followed by small-group discussion; and *buzz groups*, a structured format to talk about difficult concepts and ensure all students in large classes contribute to the discussion (McKeachie & Svinicki, 2006). Also, much of the research and dialog about active learning in college classrooms suggests that lecture, when combined with active-learning techniques, is a worthwhile alternative to a lecture-only format.

Prompt and meaningful feedback from faculty has a general positive impact on educational gains (Cole, 2008). Faculty feedback on performance has been found to be valuable across disciplines. For example, Dohrer (1991) used drafts, interviews, and think-aloud protocols to study undergraduate students' views of instructor feedback in a writing course and concluded that feedback and opportunities for revision helped students learn from their mistakes. Koprowski (1997) found that peer reviews enabled students to feel empowered by the process of giving and receiving comments and resulted in significantly improved writing in science when compared to receiving feedback from the instructor alone. (See Chapter 9 for more on assessment techniques.)

Time-on-task is perhaps the most important influence on student learning. Pace's (1979; 1980) research connecting the quality of student effort with student learning, and Astin's (1984; 1993b) theory of student involvement, which emphasizes the psychological energy that learning demands, demonstrate the importance of students' dedicating time to educationally purposeful activities, such as studying, interacting with faculty and peers, participating in campus organizations, and attending campus events. Instructional approaches are needed to encourage time-on-task, including faculty (a) clearly communicating the minimum amount of time required to prepare for class and understand complex material; (b) helping students set challenging goals for their own learning; (c) underscoring the importance of regular work, steady application, self-pacing, and scheduling; and (d) meeting with students who fall behind to discuss their study habits, schedules, and other commitments.

Communicating high expectations to all students and showing regard for their unique interests and talents facilitates academic, social, personal, and vocational growth (Sorcinelli, 1991). A key element of high expectations is adopting a talent development (Astin, 1985) philosophy throughout the institution. Such a view contends that "excellence is determined by our ability to develop the talents of our students" (Astin, 1993a, p. 6). In addition to recognizing that every student can learn under the right conditions, this perspective requires the institution to organize its resources and create conditions for teaching and learning based on educationally effective practices (Harper & Quaye, 2009; Kuh, Kinzie, Schuh, Whitt, & Associates, 2010).

Respecting diverse talents and ways of learning is appropriate for all students; however, this principle is particularly effective in working with historically underserved students, especially when their experiences, talents, and skills are honored and viewed as classroom assets. Because faculty members can at times misunderstand, ignore, or devalue the talents of students from diverse backgrounds, differences can be viewed as deficiencies (Harper & Quaye, 2009). Treisman (1992) found that African American and Hispanic students, who met academic prerequisites and demonstrated ability, failed calculus, not because of a lack of motivation (as initially presumed by faculty) but because of social and intellectual isolation (i.e., students studied alone, kept their academic and social lives separate, and were marginalized through campus programs that failed to link multiethnic student communities around shared academic interests). Through talent development strategies, these students were able to use and further hone their mathematical and problem-solving talents (Treisman, 1992). Further, engaging students in diverse learning experiences is vital to advancing student learning and gains in multicultural understanding and intercultural outcomes (Harper & Quaye, 2009). Incorporating readings that reflect the scholarly contribution of diverse writers and, more importantly, listening to diverse students in order to understand how to enhance their educational experience can help enrich the learning environment for all students, fostering greater progress in personal and educational growth (Chang, Denson, Saenz, & Misa, 2006; Hurtado, Dey, Gurin, & Gurin, 2003; Umbach & Kuh, 2006). Among the more effective approaches related to introducing diverse perspectives are using interactive teaching techniques, such as small-group discussions, role playing, and debates; creating a supportive, inclusive classroom climate; recognizing that everyone, including faculty, is a learner; and reflecting on how to use the diversity present among members of the class to enhance learning (ACE & AAUP, 2000).

Cumulative Impact of Principles

Research examining the cumulative value when students experience all seven principles has also been conducted. Kuh, Pace, and Vesper (1997) created indicators to examine three of the seven principles—student-faculty contact, cooperation among students, and active learning—and their relationship to students' self-reported learning gains in general education, intellectual skills, and personal and social development. The indicators showed positive and consistent relationships to self-reported learning outcomes. In addition, multivariate longitudinal analyses of these practices at a diverse group of 18 institutions have shown them to be related to cognitive development and several other positive outcomes (Cruce et al., 2006). Similarly, as part of their comprehensive reviews of research on college impact, Pascarella and Terenzini (1991, 2005) concluded that exposure to a range of instructional practices, such as peer teaching, active discussion, experiential learning, integration across courses, and effective teaching practices, contributes to students' engagement in learning and academic work, thereby enhancing their learning and development.

Other Good Instructional Practices

Improvements to teaching and learning require increased attention to implementing engaging pedagogies. Recent research on effective instruction and what outstanding teachers do offers practical lessons for instructional practice. Bain (2004) used observation, interviews with teachers and their students, focus groups, and reviews of course syllabi and student work to study the practices of dozens of professors who were extraordinarily successful in helping students learn in ways that made a sustained and positive influence on their learning and development. Bain concluded that outstanding teachers employed several broad patterns of thinking and practice, including (a) a conviction that teaching demands hard work and is approached thoughtfully; (b) an instructional practice built by working backwards from larger student objectives, not getting bogged down in details; (c) high expectations of students and a belief that all students want to learn and can; and (d) systems to solicit and incorporate student feedback. Most importantly, as teachers prepare, conduct, and evaluate their classes, they regard their students' learning with as much interest as their own process of discovery in their discipline.

A classic book in college pedagogy that emphasizes instructional practice and depicts the craft of teaching is *McKeachie's Teaching Tips* (Svinicki & McKeachie, 2014). This resource provides strategies for everyday teaching and suggestions to maximize learning for every student. The book summarizes current best practices succinctly and describes the most foundational aspects of teaching, including writing objectives, encouraging active learning in large classes, making group learning work, and teaching students to read actively. It also addresses concepts such as motivational theory, cultural diversity, and the ethics of teaching and learning. Because effective educational practice should help students become aware of the strategies for learning and problem solving, it is incumbent on educators to employ a range of methods to engage students, make these explicit to students, and facilitate the development and awareness of learning strategies and methods for continued learning.

Another research-based resource for instructional practice is *Tools for Teaching* (Davis, 2009). Many of the topics are similar to those addressed in *McKeachie's Teaching Tips,* including course designs that support engagement, methods to encourage participation in discussion-based classes, effective lecturing, and ways to personalize the learning experience for students. Research-based strategies, including collaborative learning, case study analysis, simulations, undergraduate research, guest speaker presentations, and civic engagement opportunities, are presented. Instructional practices that contribute to learning and occur outside the classroom are also discussed, such as making effective use of office hours, communicating with students electronically, and providing academic advising.

In *How Learning Looks: Seven Research-Based Principles for Smart Learning,* Ambrose and colleagues (2010) distilled the research literature from a breadth of perspectives, including cognitive, developmental, and social psychology as well as anthropology and organizational behavior, explicating general measures of how students learn and translating the findings into what this means for effective teaching. These key principles include (a) acknowledging students' prior knowledge, (b) using effective organization to enhance student learning, (c) applying information about what impacts motivation, (d) helping students develop and integrate component skills to develop mastery, (e) employing goal-directed practice and targeted feedback, (f) creating a positive climate to energize students' learning, and (g) teaching students how to monitor and adjust their approaches to learning to become self-directed learners. Integrating theory with real-classroom examples in practice, this resource helps faculty apply cognitive science advances to improve their own teaching.

Most resources for instructional practice emphasize the value of faculty inquiry into teaching practice, often identified in the teaching and learning literature as employing *classroom assessment techniques*, or CATs (Cross & Steadman, 1996; Steadman, 1998). This technique involves checking in with students to gauge what they are learning and what they do not fully understand as a way to improve instruction and student performance. CATs are an inquiry into what students are actually learning when they are in the process of gaining new knowledge. By systematically asking students about their learning as a normal part of a course, it is possible to gain valuable feedback about gaps in students' understanding of a particular topic. The goal is to gain an understanding of what students know (and do not know) in order to make responsive changes in teaching. CATs are anonymous, nongraded, and aimed at gathering feedback from students about what they have learned and what they find confusing about a topic. Research has examined the effects of CATs on student learning (Angelo & Cross, 1993; Cross & Steadman 1996) and found they contribute to deep learning and greater involvement in the learning process, among other outcomes.

As the resources referenced in this section demonstrate, a wealth of research-based approaches is available to instructors interested in the literature on teaching. These principles and practices can aid in the design of course; classroom pedagogy; and, more broadly, the environment for learning.

Student Engagement

The use of the term *engagement* followed from the conclusion that "the greater the student's involvement or engagement in academic work or in the academic experience of college, the greater his or her level of knowledge acquisition and general cognitive development" (Pascarella & Terenzini, 1991, p. 616). In 2005, the authors proposed that colleges and universities optimize conditions to encourage student engagement. They determined that once students start college, a key factor to whether they will survive and thrive is the extent to which they take part in educationally effective activities (Pascarella & Terenzini, 2005).

The components of educationally effective practice associated with student engagement include Chickering and Gamson's (1987) seven principles (which were discussed above), and additional student behaviors and institutional conditions proven to be associated with desirable outcomes, such as student satisfaction, persistence, educational attainment, and learning and development (Kuh, 2001, 2003; McCormick, Kinzie, & Gonyea, 2013; Pascarella, Seifert, & Blaich 2010; Pascarella & Terenzini, 1991, 2005; Pike, 1995). Student behaviors include such aspects as the time and effort students put into their studies, interaction with faculty, and peer involvement. Institutional conditions include resources and educational polices, programs, and practices. Most important about the student engagement concept is that it involves the intersection of student behaviors *and* institutional conditions. For example, high levels of purposeful student-faculty contact and active and collaborative learning supported by institutional environments perceived by students as inclusive and affirming can foster student engagement. Both student and institutional dimensions are critical to student engagement.

The advent of the National Survey of Student Engagement (NSSE) in 2000 increased the visibility of the concept of student engagement in postsecondary education. Hundreds of baccalaureate-granting institutions began to assess engagement in an intentional and empirical way, and by 2013, more than 1,500 colleges and universities had information about the quality of student engagement. The annual survey of first-year students and seniors asks students how often they have participated in, for example, projects that required integrating ideas or information from various sources; posed questions in class or contributed to class discussions; received prompt feedback from faculty on their academic performance; participated in service-learning projects; or tutored or taught other students. The questionnaire provides institutions and students a clear sense of what matters to student learning and success and can deepen institutional understanding of how students perceive learning experiences and the college environment.

An important more recent finding related to student engagement research is the evidence that certain institutional conditions, structures, and educational practices make substantial contributions to persistence, student development, and learning (NSSE, 2007; Kuh, 2008). These practices (dubbed *high-impact*), such as learning communities, undergraduate research, and service-learning, have proven to be a promising way to promote student engagement and help students achieve the learning and personal development outcomes essential for the 21st century (AAC&U, 2007; Brownell & Swaner, 2010; Kuh, 2008; Kuh & O'Donnell, 2013). High-impact practices (a) make a claim on students' time and energy in ways that may require close interaction with faculty or diverse others, (b) call upon students to apply their learning in novel situations, and (c) are correlated with deep approaches to learning (NSSE, 2007, 2012). Providing students with opportunities to apply and test what they are learning through problem solving with peers inside and outside the classroom, study abroad, internships, and capstone experiences helps them develop habits of the mind and heart that promise to stand them in good stead for a lifetime of continuous learning. For instance, Zhao and Kuh (2004) showed that students who participated in a learning community were more engaged across the board in other educationally purposeful activities compared with their counterparts who had not participated in such a program. Students interacted to a greater degree with faculty and diverse peers; studied more; and reported a stronger emphasis on higher-order cognitive activities, such as synthesizing material and analyzing problems. They also reported gaining more from their college experience.

Edgerton (2001) introduced the term *pedagogies of engagement* to describe the modes of teaching and learning needed to improve educational quality. Over the last decade, more specific models for understanding student engagement from a pedagogical standpoint have emerged. For example, Barkley (2010) developed a classroom-based model emphasizing engagement as both a process and product of the interaction between motivation and active learning. Instructional practices should set up conditions that enhance students' eagerness to learn and require students to do more of the work. Barkley profiled faculty who created such conditions and provided a large collection of student engagement techniques developed from good teaching practice literature.

Scholars, such as Gabriel (2008), explicated the value of engagement for teaching underprepared students and offered techniques to help students raise their skills so they can complete their studies. Prominent in Dweck's (2000) principles for instruction is that teachers must help students believe in their ability to learn, and that by modeling, providing feedback, and talking to students about their effort, faculty can enhance students' learning and success. Additional teaching and learning research (e.g., Ahlfeldt, Mehta, & Sellnow, 2005; Smith et al., 2005) explored classroom-based pedagogies of engagement, particularly cooperative and problem-based learning that enhances student involvement in learning, and urged faculty to consider how students engage in their college experience in both formal and informal ways. These examples of the intersection of the scholarship of teaching and learning with student engagement demonstrate the connection of student engagement to educational practice, as well as a commitment to improvement driven by classroom-based evidence and insights.

If, as Shulman (2005) asserted, "learning begins with student engagement" (p. 38), then methods for ascertaining the extent to which students are engaged in the learning process can provide helpful feedback for campus educators who wish to make an impact on student learning. With evidence from assessments of student engagement, practitioners concerned about student success gain instructive insights about their students' educational experiences and how they may be improved. For example, survey results can reveal to faculty members the extent to which students believe courses emphasize memorization or faculty provide timely feedback. Simple data points like these can catalyze discussions about course assignments and learning assessments, or about expectations for feedback (Kuh et al., 2010).

Environments That Foster Educational Success

The quality of the total learning environment plays a role in shaping student behavior and influencing educational growth. Person-environment theory focuses on the college environment and how it influences behavior through interactions with the student. Strange and Banning (2001) classified existing environmental models, explaining how they shape student behaviors and what aspects of the environment optimize learning. They reported that educational environments are powerful when they offer students a sense of security and inclusion, mechanisms for involvement, and an experience of community.

The notion of creating a *learning-centered environmen*t (Doyle, 2008; Tagg, 2003) draws on person-environment theories, emphasizing a broad array of activities and aspects of environmental design that advance learning. Specifically, the concept shifts away from instruction that is fundamentally teacher-centered, sometimes termed *sage on the stage*, and instead emphasizes a practice in which students and professors coconstruct the learning experience and learn from one another. Learner-centered refers to environments that pay attention to the knowledge, skills, attitudes, and beliefs that learners bring to the educational setting. Weimer (2002) specified that in learning-centered environments, students are challenged to have ownership in the learning experience, including design of the curriculum, responsibility for some levels of instruction, and peer review.

Closing Call to Action: Using Research-Based Approaches to Inform Teaching

Greater attention to ensuring the success of all students and, in particular, addressing graduation rate gaps demands improvements in the conditions for learning and quality of instruction. Digital-media savvy students and increased populations of online and adult learners compel a major shift in educational methods, away from passive, lecture courses and towards interactive, collaborative learning experiences, using a variety of learning media and sites. The demand to ensure success for a wider range of students and for greater incorporation of interactive and application experiences makes it increasingly important to ensure that educational practices are aligned with these goals.

The good news is that faculty and administrators in colleges and universities seem to be interested in teaching and improving the quality of learning (Tagg, 2012). Greater attention to educational quality calls for faculty to explicitly consider how students engage in their college experience and to create learning activities that are in harmony with research findings about the best ways to help students learn. Research must inform instructional practice and the creation of successful learning experiences in more colleges and universities.

The best way to assess the value of the models and strategies suggested in this chapter and throughout this volume is to try them out. Educators may understandably feel uneasy about departing from accustomed teaching patterns, trying new strategies, or requiring more of students in terms of peer teaching. They may also worry that new pedagogy will take too much time to arrange and implement. Yet, these approaches are sound and worth the venture in terms of the potential improvement to learning as well as the feedback it provides on effectiveness. If a new method produces desired results, the next step is to determine how to make it a part of the teaching repertoire; if not, the question becomes, What needs to change, or is there a different approach? With the demand for educational reform, educators need to respond by doing something different and collect more information about what is feasible and, even more, what works.

References

Ahlfeldt, S., Mehta, S., & Sellnow, T. (2005). Measurement and analysis of student engagement in university classes where varying levels of PBL methods of instruction are in use. *Higher Education Research & Development, 24*(1), 5-20.

Ambrose, S. A., Bridges, M. W., DiPietro, M., Lovett, M. C., & Norman, M. K. (2010). *How learning works: Seven research-based principles for smart teaching.* San Francisco, CA: Jossey Bass.

American Council on Education (ACE) & American Association of University Professors (AAUP). (2000). *Does diversity make a difference? Three research studies on diversity in college classrooms* (Executive Summary). Washington, DC: Author.

Angelo, T. A., & Cross, P. K. (1993). *Classroom assessment techniques: A handbook for college teachers* (2nd ed.). San Francisco, CA: Jossey-Bass.

Association of American Colleges and Universities (AAC&U). (2007). *College learning for the new global century: A report from the National Leadership Council for Liberal Education and America's Promise.* Washington, DC: Author.

Astin, A. W. (1984). Student involvement: A developmental theory for higher education. *Journal of College Student Personnel, 25,* 297-308.

Astin, A. W. (1985). *Achieving educational excellence.* San Francisco, CA: Jossey-Bass.

Astin, A. W. (1993a). *Assessment for excellence: The philosophy and practice of assessment and evaluation in higher education.* Phoenix, AZ: American Council of Education and The Oryx Press.

Astin, A. W. (1993b). *What matters in college? Four critical years revisited.* San Francisco, CA: Jossey-Bass.

Bain, K. (2004). *What the best college teachers do.* Cambridge, MA: Harvard University Press.

Barkley, E. F. (2010). *Student engagement techniques: A handbook for college faculty.* San Francisco, CA: Jossey-Bass.

Berger, J., & Milem, J. (2000). Organizational behavior in higher education and student-outcomes. In J. C. Smart (Ed.), *Higher education: Handbook of theory and research* (Vol. XV, pp. 268-338). New York, NY: Agathon.

Bonwell, C. C., & Eison, J. A. (1991). *Active learning: Creating excitement in the classroom* (ASHE-ERIC Higher Education Report No. 1). Washington, DC: Association for the Study of Higher Education.

Bransford, J., Brown, A., & Cocking, R., (2000). *How people learn: Brain, mind, experience, and school.* (2nd ed.). Washington, D.C.: National Academy Press.

Braxton, J. M., Jones, W. A., Hirschy, A. S., & Hartley, H. V., III. (2008). The role of active learning in college persistence. *New Directions for Teaching and Learning, 115*, 71-83.

Brownell, J. E., & Swaner, L. E. (2010). *Five high-impact practices: Research on learning outcomes, completion, and quality.* Washington, DC: Association of American Colleges & University.

Chang, M. J., Denson, N., Saenz, V., & Misa, K. (2006) The educational benefits of sustaining cross-racial interaction among undergraduates. *Journal of Higher Education, 77*(3), 430-455.

Chickering, A. W., & Gamson, Z. (1987). Seven principles for good practice in undergraduate education. *American Association for Higher Education Bulletin, 39*(7), 3-7.

Chickering, A. W., & Gamson, Z. F. (1991). *Applying the seven principles for good practice in undergraduate education.* San Francisco, CA: Jossey-Bass.

Cole, D. (2008). Constructive criticism: The role of faculty feedback on African American and Hispanic students' educational gains. *Journal of College Student Development, 49*(6), 587-605.

Cross, K. P., & Steadman, M. (1996). *Classroom research.* San Francisco, CA: Jossey-Bass.

Cruce, T. M., Wolniak, G. C., Seifert, T. A., & Pascarella, E. T. (2006). Impacts of good practices on cognitive development, learning orientations, and graduate degree plans during the first year of college. *Journal of College Student Development, 47*(4), 365-383.

Davis, B. G. (2009). *Tools for teaching* (2nd ed.). San Francisco, CA: Jossey-Bass.

Delaney, A. M. (2008). Why faculty-student interaction matters in the first year experience. *Tertiary Education and Management, 14*(3), 227-241.

Dohrer, G. (1991). Do teachers' comments on students' papers help? *College Teaching, 39*(2), 48-54.

Doyle, T. (2008). *Helping students learning in a learner-centered environment: A guide to facilitating learning in higher education.* Sterling, VA: Stylus.

Durrington, V. A., Berryhill, A., & Swafford, J. (2006). Strategies for enhancing student interactivity in an online environment. *College Teaching, 54*(1), 190-193.

Dweck, C. S. (2000). *Self-theories: Their role in motivation, personality, and development.* Philadelphia, PA: Psychology Press.

Edgerton, R. (2001). *Education white paper.* (Report prepared for the Pew Charitable Trusts, Pew Forum on Undergraduate Learning). Washington, DC: Pew Charitable Trusts.

Education Commission of the States (1995). *Making quality count in undergraduate education. A report for the ECS chairman's "quality counts" agenda in higher education.* Denver, CO: Education Commission of the States.

Faust, J. L., & Paulson, D. R. (1998). Active learning in the college classroom. *Journal on Excellence in College Teaching, 9*(2), 3-24.

Gabriel, K. F. (2008). *Teaching underprepared students: Strategies for promoting success and retention in higher education.* Sterling, VA: Stylus.

Graunke, S. S., & Woosley, S. A. (2005). An exploration of the factors that affect the academic success of college sophomores. *College Student Journal, 39*(2), 367-377.

Hake, R. R. (1998). Interactive engagement vs. traditional methods: A six thousand-student survey of mechanics test data for introductory physics courses. *American Journal of Physics, 66*, 64-75.

Harper, S. R., & Quaye, S. J. (Eds.). (2009). *Student engagement in higher education: Theoretical perspectives and practical approaches for diverse populations.* New York, NY: Routledge.

Hurtado, S., Dey, E. L., Gurin, P. Y., & Gurin, G. (2003). College environments, diversity, and student learning. In J. C. Smart (Ed.), *Higher education: Handbook of theory and research,* (Vol. 13, pp. 145-189). Boston, MA: Kluwer Academic Publishers.

Juillerat, S. (2000). Assessing the expectations and satisfactions of sophomores. In L. A. Schreiner & J. Pattengale (Eds.), *Visible solutions for invisible students: Helping sophomores succeed* (Monograph 31, pp.19-29). Columbia, SC: University of South Carolina, National Resource Center for The First-Year Experience & Students in Transition.

Koprowski, J. L. (1997). Honing the craft of scientific writing: The role of peer review. *Journal of College Science Teaching, 27*, 133-135.

Koprowski, J. L., & Perigo, N. (2000). Cooperative learning as a tool to teach vertebrate anatomy. *American Biology Teacher, 26*, 282-284.

Kuh, G. D. (2001). Assessing what really matters to student learning: Inside the National Survey of Student Engagement. *Change, 33*(3), 10-17.

Kuh, G. D. (2003). What we're learning about student engagement from NSSE. *Change, 35*(2), 24-32.

Kuh, G. D. (2008). *High-Impact educational practices: What they are, who has access to them, and why they matter.* Washington, DC: Association of American Colleges and Universities.

Kuh, G. D., & Hu, S. (2001) The effects of student faculty interaction in the 1990s. *Review of Higher Education, 24*(3), 309-332.

Kuh, G. D., Kinzie, J., Schuh, J. H., Whitt, E. J., & Associates (2010). *Student success in college: Creating conditions that matter.* San Francisco, CA: Jossey-Bass.

Kuh, G. D., & O'Donnell, K. (2013). *Ensuring quality and taking high-impact practices to scale.* Washington, DC: Association of American Colleges and Universities.

Kuh, G. D., Pace, C. R., & Vesper, N. (1997). The development of process indicators to estimate student gains associated with good practices in undergraduate education. *Research in Higher Education, 38*(4), 435-454.

Ladson-Billings, G. (1995). Toward a theory of culturally relevant pedagogy. *American Educational Research Journal 32*, 465-491.

Lundberg, C. A., & Schreiner, L. A. (2004). Quality and frequency of faculty-student interaction as predictors of learning: An analysis by student race/ethnicity. *Journal of College Student Development, 45*(5), 549-565.

Mayhew, M. J., Wolniak, G. C., & Pascarella, E. T. (2008). How educational practices affect the development of life-long learning orientations in traditionally-aged undergraduate students. *Research in Higher Education, 49*, 337-356.

McCormick, A. C., Kinzie, J., & Gonyea, R. M. (2013). Student engagement: Bridging research and practice to improve the quality of undergraduate education. In M. B. Paulsen (Ed.), *Higher education: Handbook of theory and research* (Vol. 28, pp. 47-92). Dordrecht, The Netherlands: Springer.

McKeachie, W. J., & Svinicki, M. (2006). *McKeachie's teaching tips: Strategies, research, and theory for college and university teachers* (12th ed.). Boston, MA: Houghton Mifflin.

Michaelsen, L. K., Knight, A. B., & Fink, L. D. (2004). *Team-based learning: A transformative use of small groups in college teaching.* Sterling, VA: Stylus.

National Survey of Student Engagement (NSSE). (2007). *Experiences that matter: Enhancing student learning and success.* Bloomington, IN: Indiana University Center for Postsecondary Research.

National Survey of Student Engagement (NSSE). (2012). *Moving from data to action: Lessons from the field* (Vol. 2). Bloomington, IN: Indiana University Center for Postsecondary Research.

Pace, C. R. (1979). *Measuring outcomes of college: Fifty years of findings and recommendations for the future.* San Francisco, CA: Jossey-Bass.

Pace, C. R. (1980). Measuring the quality of student effort. *Current Issues in Higher Education, 2*, 10-16.

Pascarella, E. T., & Blaich, C. (2013). Lessons from the Wabash National Study of Liberal Arts Education. *Change, 45*(2), 6-15.

Pascarella, E. T., Salisbury, M. H., & Blaich, C. (2011). Exposure to effective instruction and college student persistence: A multi-institutional replication and extension. *Journal of College Student Development, 52*(1), 4-19.

Pascarella, E. T., Seifert, T. A., & Blaich, C. (2010). How effective are the NSSE benchmarks in predicting important educational outcomes? *Change 42*(1), 16-22.

Pascarella, E. T., & Terenzini, P. T. (1991). *How college affects students: Findings and insights from twenty years of research.* San Francisco, CA: Jossey-Bass.

Pascarella, E. T., & Terenzini, P. T. (2005). *How college affects students: A third decade of research* (Vol. 2). San Francisco, CA: Jossey-Bass.

Pike, G. R. (1995). The relationships between self reports of college experiences and achievement test scores. *Research in Higher Education, 36*, 1-22.

Pintrich, P. R. (2002). The role of metacognitive knowledge in learning, teaching, and assessing. *Theory into Practice, 41*(4), 219-225.

Reason, R. D., Terenzini, P. T., & Domingo, R. J. (2006). First things first: Developing academic competence in the first year of college. *Research in Higher Education, 47*(2), 149-175.

Shulman, L. S. (2005). Making differences: A table of learning. *Change, 34*(6), 36-44.

Silberman, M. (1996). *Active learning: 101 strategies to teach any subject.* Boston, MA: Allyn & Bacon.

Slavin, R. E. (1990). *Cooperative learning: Theories, research, and practice.* Englewood Cliffs, NJ: Prentice-Hall.

Smith, K. A., Sheppard, S. D., Johnson, D. W., & Johnson, R. T. (2005). Pedagogies of engagement: Classroom-based practices. *Journal of Engineering Education, 94*(1), 87-102.

Sorcinelli, M. D. (1991). Research findings on the seven principles. *New Directions for Teaching and Learning, 47,* 13-25.

Sousa, D. (2011). *How the brain learns* (4th ed.). Thousand Oaks, CA: Corwin Press.

Steadman, M. H. (1998). CATs: Using classroom assessment to change both teaching and learning. *New Directions for Teaching and Learning, 75,* 23-35.

Strange, C. C., & Banning, J. H. (2001) *Educating by design: Creating campus learning environments that work.* San Francisco, CA: Jossey-Bass.

Svinicki, M., & McKeachie, W. J. (2014). *McKeachie's teaching tips: Strategies, research, and theory for college and university teachers.* (14th ed.). Belmont, CA: Wadsworth.

Tagg, J. (2003). *The learning paradigm college.* Bolton, MA: Anker.

Tagg, J. (2012). Why does the faculty resist change? *Change, 44,* 6-15.

Treisman, U. (1992). Studying students studying calculus: A look at the lives of minority mathematics students in college. *College Mathematics Journal, 23*(5), 362-372.

Umbach, P. D., & Kuh, G. D. (2006). Student experiences with diversity at liberal arts colleges: Another claim for distinctiveness. *Journal of Higher Education, 77*(1), 169-192.

Umbach, P. D., & Wawrzynski, M. R. (2005). Faculty do matter: The role of college faculty in student learning and engagement. *Research in Higher Education, 46*(2), 153-184.

Weimer, M. (2002). *Learner-centered teaching.* San Francisco, CA: Wiley.

Zambreno, K., Hoover, E., Anderson, N., & Gillman, J. H. (2002). *Writing across the curriculum: Where does horticultural science fit in?* (Center for Interdisciplinary Studies of Writing Technical Report Series No. 19). Minneapolis, MN: The University of Minnesota, Center for Interdisciplinary Studies of Writing.

Zhao, C. M., & Kuh, G. D., (2004). Adding value: Learning communities and student engagement. *Research in Higher Education, 45*(2), 115-138.

Zull, J. (2002) *The art of changing the brain.* Sterling, VA: Stylus.

Chapter 3
Historical Overview of Learning Theories

James E. Groccia, Stacey C. Nickson, Chenzi Wang, and Heather Hardin

A basic understanding of learning theories can improve teaching. Specifically, knowledge of learning theories as conceptual frameworks that describe how information is acquired, processed, and retained through cognitive, emotional, environmental, and experiential influences can strategically guide instructors in meeting the needs of learners and choosing from a variety of teaching methods to best reach specific learning outcomes (Snowman, McCown, & Biehler, 2009). This chapter begins with an overview of learning theories, addressing their development, importance, and role in teaching and learning. Of the many theories on human learning, six have been selected for a more in-depth presentation due to their influence in shaping pedagogical practice in U.S. colleges and universities: (a) behaviorism, (b) cognitivism, (c) constructivism, (d) humanism, (e) transformational learning, and (f) andragogy. For each discussion, a summary is offered followed by general teaching applications grounded in that theory.

Overview of Learning Theories

Learning is a complex process that has long vexed philosophers, psychologists, educators, anthropologists, linguists, neurophysiologists, and others trying to understand how the mind works and how people learn (Phillips & Soltis, 2004). Those seeking to understand learning have drawn from numerous sources (Gredler, 1992), such as philosophy (e.g., logical assumptions about the nature of human behavior and reality) and traditional wisdom (e.g., proverbs and maxims based on observation of human experience).

Theory is another tool for understanding how people learn. Gredler (1992) defined theory as an organized set of principles about particular events in the environment. Dimitriadis and Kamberelis (2006) further elaborated on this definition by noting that theories are sets of assumptions and assertions that can be used to interpret, explain, and apply psychological, social, cultural, and historical processes. They help us think about things in new ways, providing avenues for innovation and creativity, and offering a conceptual framework that can be used to understand, integrate, and test items of interest. A unique characteristic of learning theories, in particular, is that they focus on the underlying (and unobservable) psychological dynamics of events, providing a way to understand learning in both formal and informal settings (Gredler, 1992). The following sections will discuss selected families of theories in more detail.

Behaviorism

From the 1920s until the 1950s, behaviorism was the dominant theory in psychology and education (Gredler, 1992). It was a first attempt to go beyond the study of internal mental processes (e.g., structuralism, functionalism, Freudian psychology) and focus on behavior as the key to understanding human learning. John B. Watson (1913) argued that learning was the result of patterns of responses to external stimuli. He claimed

> Give me a dozen healthy infants, well formed, and my own specified world to bring them up in, and I'll guarantee to take any one at random and train him to become any type of specialist I might select—doctor, lawyer, artist, merchant-chief—regardless of his talents, penchants, tendencies, abilities, vocations, and race of his ancestors. (Watson, 1925, p. 65)

Watson's view of learning integrated both Ivan Pavlov's (1927) *classical conditioning* and Edward Lee Thorndike's (1911) *instrumental conditioning*. Pavlov's research demonstrated how naturally occurring behaviors or reflexes could be learned when paired with previously neutral stimuli, resulting in new behaviors. For example, a dog automatically salivates when presented a bowl of food (unconditioned stimulus). After repeated pairings of food with the sound of a bell (a neutral stimulus), the dog learns to salivate to the bell's sound even without the presentation of food. On the other hand, Thorndike highlighted the connection between particular stimuli and voluntary behaviors. In his experiments observing how animals learn to escape from a box (i.e., by pressing a lever to open the door and receive a food reward), he found that, over time, the number of wrong responses (i.e., random movements not resulting in a pressed lever) declined until the animal learned to immediately press the lever to open the door (the correct response). Thorndike (1906) called this *the law of effect,* which states that behaviors followed by positive outcomes are strengthened and behaviors followed by negative outcomes are weakened. He concluded that problem solving (learning) involved establishing associations or connections between stimuli and appropriate responses.

B. F. Skinner's (1938, 1953) version of behaviorism, *operant conditioning,* builds upon Pavlov, Thorndike, and Watson and is based on the fact that the frequency, duration, and intensity of voluntary behaviors are strengthened when they are followed by a positive consequence and weakened when they are ignored or punished. In other words, people learn or unlearn new behavior through patterns of reinforcement (positive or negative) or punishments. Applied to classroom situations, operant conditioning provides instructors with overt, observable tools to shape student learning toward desired outcomes by

- offering reward or reinforcement when students succeed and withholding reward when students are unsuccessful at achieving desired learning outcomes;
- moving from rewarding every instance of student success to an intermittent reward schedule, building motivation and encouraging students to work even when not rewarded as they know reinforcement will follow continued learning effort; and
- developing individualized learning plans, allowing students to progress at their own rate and where success in one task leads to the next task.

Behaviorism is often linked to "status quo methods and conditions such as teacher-centered classrooms, lectures, and passive reception of material" (Wilson & Myers, 2000, p. 60). A detailed description of behaviorism's influence on teaching and learning is beyond the scope of this chapter (see Cook, 1997; Glover & Ronning, 1987); however, according to Wilson and Myers (2000), behaviorism has contributed the following insights and suggestions for enhancing the design of effective learning environments:

- People learn best by practice and actively engaging in learning tasks.
- Instruction should be based on clear, behaviorally specified learning outcomes.
- Teachers and schools should be accountable for their students' learning. Measurable behaviors are the best index of learning outcomes and should be used to gauge instructional effectiveness.
- Good instruction exhibits an alignment or consistency between learning objectives, instructional strategies, and assessments of student learning. Misalignment of these components results in inadequate or unfair instruction.
- People learn best when complex tasks are broken down into smaller, more manageable tasks. Further, students learn the larger tasks more easily when they have first mastered the smaller tasks.
- Succeeding at tasks is reinforcing, resulting in greater motivation to continue learning efforts.
- People learn best when they know the correctness of their efforts. When performance is not correct, specific information should be conveyed concerning what was wrong and how to improve the next time.
- Giving clear directions, well-prepared presentations, examples, and opportunities for practice and transfer are proven methods that result in substantial student learning.
- Students should not all be forced to endure the same instructional program. Instead, instruction should branch into alternative treatments according to prior skills, motivations, and other critical variables.

Behavioral psychologists, such as Pavlov, Thorndike, Watson, and Skinner, viewed learning primarily as the acquisition and strengthening of responses (Mayer, 1992). The goal of behavioral instruction is to have learners respond correctly to stimuli (Ertmer & Newby, 1993). Instruction requires the teacher to select stimuli to which learners respond and divide material to be learned into small tasks that can be easily mastered (Schunk, 2000).

Cognitivism

Cognitive theories of learning have their origins in Germany during the first decade of the 20th century. Early German cognitive psychologists did not believe behaviorism fully accounted for student learning, even though they acknowledged the role of the environment in facilitating learning, such as when students use a teacher's explanations and actions as cues for their responses (Pintrich, Cross, Kozma, & McKeachie, 1986). They contended, unlike behaviorists, that learning is an internal mental process that can be inferred from what people do and say. To understand human learning, cognitivists focus on how information is acquired, constructed, organized, encoded, rehearsed, stored, and retrieved from memory. Cognitivism states that learners are active interpreters and controllers of environmental stimuli, not simply controlled responders. What students do with information (i.e., the degree to which they study and use it) is most critical to learning.

A variant of cognitive learning theory—*information-processing theory*—highlights how people attend to, recognize, transform, store, and retrieve information (Snowman et al., 2009). Information processing theory proposes an internal model of learning through a series of storage and retrieval processes. Concepts like short-term and long-term memory are introduced here. The theory contends information is stored just long enough for unconscious mental processes to analyze it and determine whether the input should be brought into working or short-term memory, or discarded. Short-term memory is limited in capacity (the amount of information stored), duration (how long information can be retained or remembered before it is forgotten), and speed of processing (how quickly information can be retrieved). Memory capacity, duration, and speed all increase with maturation and experience. Through the learner-controlled processes of attention, recognition of meaningfulness, practice, rehearsal, and retrieval, information in short-term memory is encoded into long-term memory. Akin to a hard drive in a computer, long-term memory keeps information that is not currently being used for an indefinite period of time. Applying information-processing theory to teaching suggests that instructors (a) develop ways to help students pay attention to what is to be learned; (b) divide learning tasks into organized, meaningful, manageable chunks or bits of information; (c) break class learning activities into 15-20 minute units; (d) present important information at the beginning or end of the lesson when attention is highest; and (e) use concrete examples to help make learning meaningful to students.

Jean Piaget also occupies a central position in the development of cognitive learning theories (Snowman et al., 2009). His concept of learning is centered on *equilibration,* where learning results from the individual's efforts to maintain mental balance through an active process of adapting to new environmental stimuli (Illeris, 2004). Learning occurs through the balancing of two mental processes: (a) *assimilation* of new information into existing mental frameworks or knowledge and (b) *accommodation* of mental frameworks to accept new information. Therefore, learning is a process of constant elaboration, clarification, construction, and reconstruction of existing knowledge in the face of new information. Teaching strategies suggested by Piaget's theories include creating cognitive controversies, using ethical dilemma and debate, and scaffolding new information to create manageable disequilibrium to motivate student learning.

Occupying a midpoint between behaviorism and cognitive learning theories, *social cognitive learning theory* shares principles with both and emphasizes how behavioral and personal factors interact with the social setting in which behavior occurs (Snowman et al., 2009). Albert Bandura (1986, 2002), the chief proponent of this theory, suggested that learning occurs through reciprocal interactions among three factors: (a) personal characteristics, self-perceptions, and emotions; (b) behaviors; and (c) interactions with others. Central to social cognitive theories is the role of observation and modeling in learning. Students can learn by simply observing another perform a behavior without direct reinforcement of their own behavior.

Applying this theory to teaching suggests the instructor's goal is to facilitate learner self-control and self-regulation. That is, to develop learning activities that reinforce student motivation so students become responsible for their own learning. Cognitive theories focus on what learners know and how they come to know it (i.e., the thinking process), and there is less concern with what learners do (i.e., the behavioral approach). Teaching practices based on cognitive learning theories stress active involvement by students, emphasizing the structure and organization of knowledge and linking new knowledge to learners' prior cognitive structures (Ertmer & Newby, 1993). Techniques that build upon cognitive learning theory include the use of concept maps, mnemonic devices, and advanced organizers.

Constructivism

Constructivism posits that learning happens by assigning (i.e., constructing) meaning to new information based on one's prior knowledge and experience (Alexander & Winne, 2006; Matthews, 2003; Svinicki, 2004; Taylor & MacKenney, 2008). Constructivist learning theory emphasizes the connections students make between their many ideas about the world contextualized with their personal experiences and views (Alexander & Winne, 2006).

While this theory is viewed as emerging in the late-20th century, constructivism's origins can be traced to prior centuries (Warrick, 2001). For example, elements of constructivism can be found in Rousseau's 18th century developmentalist thoughts, which held that learning is nurtured by allowing mental and emotional growth to occur as an organic course of affairs (Matthews, 2003). It is also seen in John Dewey's progressive education movement in the United States (1896-1904) that claimed education's purpose was to provide context for the natural interests and characteristics of students (Gage & Berliner, 1998; Matthews, 2003; Ornstein & Levine, 2008; Warrick, 2001).

While these and other theorists and researchers (e.g., Maria Montessori, Jerome Bruner, David Kolb) have contributed to constructivist learning theory, the work of Lev Vygotsky is considered most significant to its development (Alexander & Winne, 2006; Gage & Berliner, 1998; Matthews, 2003; Ornstein & Levine, 2008; Taylor & MacKenney, 2008; Warrick, 2001). Vygotsky's sociocultural approach proposes that culture is a major influence on learning (Taylor & MacKenney, 2008). He saw a direct correlation between intellectual ability and culture, in that culture provides both the information and the process (e.g., structured or unstructured classroom environments) through which we learn (Woolfolk, 2001). Culture also determines our access to tools, both real (e.g., calendars, rulers, smartphones) and symbolic (e.g., number systems, alphabets), and those tools directly support our thinking and learning skills (Woolfolk, 2001). Vygotsky identified learning as occurring in the *zone of proximal development,* which is the space between what learners are able to do independently and what they can do through interactions with a teacher and/or peers within a supportive learning environment (Alexander & Winne, 2006). For example, when a teacher is able to identify a child's current knowledge level and, therefore, provide learning opportunities that consider his or her age, experience, and prior knowledge (a process called *scaffolding*), the young learner will be operating in his or her zone of proximal development (Alexander & Winne, 2006).

A constructivist classroom shifts the focus from the instructor to the student since the active involvement of students becomes paramount to learning (Taylor & MacKenney, 2008). The model of the teacher as the sole expert is replaced by expectations of student-created-and-acquired knowledge and expertise. A student's current knowledge is also valued as contributing to knowledge construction of other students in the learning environment (Alexander & Winne, 2006). Students are free to personalize the results of their learning as they have responsibility for developing, modifying, and ultimately accepting new knowledge (Gage & Berliner, 1998). In a constructivist classroom, learning is based on problem solving, and the instructor's role is to create an environment where students actively participate in investigative inquiry, take responsibility for their knowledge acquisition, and become authentic critical thinkers (Woolfolk, 2001).

Two key elements in applying the constructivist approach are for instructors (a) to emphasize teaching for the purpose of understanding and (b) to make certain that all tasks in which students engage are meaningful (Gage & Berliner, 1998). Reflective learning activities, such as writing or journaling, are encouraged to assist student recognition and understanding of their thinking and problem-solving processes. Instructors should facilitate access to resources (e.g., information, thinking, and communication tools) that will support high achievement and attainment of learning goals (Alexander & Winne, 2006). The classroom needs to be structured to promote responsibility by emphasizing student roles, group decision making, and peer discourse for appropriate interaction (Svinicki, 2004).

Authentic, project-based activities with aspects of real-world application lend themselves to students' intrinsic motivation and constructivist learning (Gage & Berliner, 1998). Activities, tasks, and projects that acknowledge students' feelings, thinking, interests, and beliefs are affectively engaging and can promote higher levels of involvement (Taylor & MacKenney, 2008). Constructivist theories also support discussion and group approaches that facilitate sharing, critiquing one's understanding, and learning from others. When students work cooperatively with structure, roles, and opportunities for leadership and are given choices in assignments or methodology, then initiative, engagement, and learning are promoted (Svinicki, 2004).

Humanism

Humanism is broadly defined by many scholars as a theoretical perspective that focuses on what individuals are capable of, their potential, their concerns, and the means by which they seek to control their lives (Schunk, 2000; Taylor & MacKenney, 2008; Woolfolk, 2001). Unlike the previous theories, it focuses on the role of noncognitive variables in learning, specifically student needs, emotions, values, and self-perceptions (Snowman et al., 2009). In this school of thought, the person is studied as a whole being (e.g., mind, emotions, social interactions) who possesses an intrinsic motivation towards self-development (Huitt, 2009; Woolfolk, 2001).

The roots of humanism can be found in the writings of Socrates, Plato, Aristotle, and Quintilian, and it served as the theoretical pillar of Greek and Roman educational institutions (Ornstein & Levine, 2008). Its influence waxed and waned through the centuries, finding a new voice in the humanist-centric progressive education movement in 20th century America, which promoted social reform through universal education policies, thus allowing humanism to have a pervasive effect in elementary to higher education (Koopman, 1987).

Modern scholars with the greatest influence on humanism's application to education are Carl Rogers and Abraham Maslow (Ornstein & Levine, 2008; Schunk, 2000; Taylor & MacKenney, 2008; Woolfolk, 2001). Rogers used his research in psychology to develop a theory of *person-centered* teaching (a term that replaced humanistic education), emphasizing the teacher as a facilitator who exhibits caring, empathy, and authenticity with students (Huitt, 2009). Maslow's research on the psychology of motivation influenced humanism's focus on intrinsic motivation in education (Woolfolk, 2001).

Rogers noted that students are in a continuous state of personal development to achieve wholeness, a process called the *actualizing tendency* (Schunk, 2000). Though this tendency is innate, the classroom environment can have a positive or negative effect since it is one place where students develop an understanding of their strengths and weaknesses (Taylor & MacKenney, 2008). Those given unconditional positive regard (acceptance) undergo growth in the actualizing tendency, while those experiencing conditional regard (acceptance only under certain circumstances) may feel less valued and not as worthy as others, slowing or preventing self-actualization (Schunk, 2000). According to Rogers, a humanist approach using non-lecture-based, student-centered, facilitative teaching, with a focus on instructor-student relationships and the promotion of student independence and self-acceptance, aids students in meeting their psychological needs within a conducive learning environment (Ornstein & Levine, 2008).

Maslow's humanistic conceptualization of motivation was hierarchical, ranging from the lowest level, physical (safety and security), to the highest level, aesthetic (self-actualization), with affiliation (social needs) and achievement (intellectual needs) in between (Gage & Berliner, 1998). This hierarchy of needs as applied to education suggests that students must have their physical needs (e.g., food, clothing, shelter, safety) met in order to operate at higher levels that support affiliation (e.g., feelings of belonging and self-esteem) and lead to the achievement (i.e., learning) level (Woolfolk, 2001). Furthermore, both the physical and affiliation needs should be positively addressed to maximize student motivation for achievement, without which self-actualization is not possible (Gage & Berliner, 1998).

Pedagogies based on this theory reflect humanist principles and objectives, such as showing positive regard and empathy for students (Schunk, 2001) and promoting the development of their social and affective skills (Huitt, 2009). Humanist teaching strategies include offering self-selected assignments and cooperative learning opportunities that diminish competition between students while increasing collaboration (Huitt, 2009; Ornstein & Levine, 2008: See Chapter 7 for more on cooperative and collaborative learning). Other techniques such as discussion promote many humanistic learning outcomes, like critical thinking, higher order learning, positive shifts in attitudes, persuasive speaking, logic, and civic engagement (Gage & Berliner, 1998). When applying humanistic learning theory, instructors strive to stimulate student self-awareness and develop a classroom environment that is supportive and nonthreatening where students can actively fulfill their natural need to learn and achieve their fullest human potential. Instructors are facilitators, encouraging choice and personal control of learning and using student-centered teaching approaches.

Transformative Learning Theory

The theory of transformative learning, developed by Jack Mezirow (1998), proposes that adult learners use their prior knowledge base to construe a new or revised interpretation of the meaning of their experience in order to guide future learning and action. Transformative learning is often triggered by a disorienting dilemma or unforeseen event that evokes "critical self-reflection, social interactions, planning for action, and building competence and self-confidence in new roles and relationships as a result of taking action" (D'Amato & Krasny, 2011, p. 239). Further, it is that reflective practice that transforms the learners' prior experience into a new frame of reference (Mezirow, 1998).

While Mezirow's theory mainly focused on how an individual's perspective affects cognitive conflicts in experience, Robert Boyd's (1991) research in this field explored how conflicts within the individual's consciousness and judgment also lead to "fundamental change in one's personality" (as cited in Taylor, 1998, p. 13). During transformative learning, an individual remains open to listening to alternative interpretations and expressions of meaning before choosing a viewpoint (Boyd & Myers, 1988). Further, the individual becomes aware of the limitations and possibilities of old and new patterns of thinking and seeks to integrate them both (Imel, 1998). Mentors and teachers play very important roles in this transformation by helping students confront the limitations of their previous ways of knowing and engage in the process of whole person learning (Stevens-Long, Schapiro, & McClintock, 2012).

Paolo Freire (1984) supported the centrality of critical reflection and viewed transformative learning as a social learning process. Edward Taylor (1998, 2008), however, noted that learners may need help developing their awareness and ability to transform society and their own reality; therefore, educators should build student-teacher relationships and offer a safe educational atmosphere where they can talk and share with students to facilitate consciousness-raising and transformational learning. Educators must also challenge learners to think more critically while supporting them in their difficult explorations. Instructors can create maximally transformative learning by offering high-challenge and high-support learning environments using critical questions, consciousness-raising simulations and experiential exercises, reflective journal writing, and content-based critical incidents for reflection (Cranton, 1994; Daloz, 1986).

Andragogy

According to Knowles (1980), *andragogy* is "the art and science of helping adult learning" (p. 43). Introduced by Alexander Kapp in 1883, the term andragogy was not used in the mainstream of educational theory for almost 90 years until educators, Eugen Rosenstorck-Huessy and Eduard Lindeman, re-examined andragogy as a concept of adult education in 1926. In the 1950s, Malcolm Knowles expanded andragogy from a model to a theory of adult learning (Boeve, 2012; Chan, 2010; Zmeyov, 1998). With the increasing number of nontraditional, adult learners in higher education during recent decades, the principles of andragogy can help ground the development of student learning outcomes and initiatives addressing the needs of today's college students (Boeve, 2012; Goddu, 2012; Houle, 1996; Hoyt, Howell, Touchet, Young, & Wygant, 2010; Merriam, 2001; Merriam & Caffarella, 1991; Ross-Gordon, 2011).

Knowles (1980) described andragogy as consisting of four essential assumptions: learners (a) are self-directed; (b) have rich prior experiences that become a valuable resource for learning; (c) are ready to learn the developmental tasks of social roles; and (d) are eager to learn information that is readily applicable to their lives. Further, adults are inclined to be more internally, rather than externally, motivated and tend to need to know why they must acquire new knowledge (Keesee, 2010; Knowles, Holton, & Swanson, 1998; Merriam, Caffarella, & Baumgartner, 2007). According to McGrath (2009), adult learning theory proposes that instructors are no longer the center of the classroom and that students should be encouraged to interact with their teachers and classmates by using their own experiences. Educators of adult learners must "involve learners in as many aspects of their education as possible and in the creation of a climate in which both they and the students can fruitfully learn" (Houle, 1996, p. 30).

Mahdi and Bright (2010), while addressing adult learning specifically, offered teaching applications appropriate for all learners. They suggested faculty members take time during and after class to facilitate sharing of experiences and insights through "active listening, skillful paraphrasing, describing experiences and behavior without judgment, and engaging people with unconditional positive regard" (Mahdi & Bright, 2010, p. 21). In addition, interpersonal interactions should be facilitated on a reasonably regular basis to provide opportunity for mutual understanding of behavior and intentions. Instructors must also be empathetic, willing to create a safe learning environment, and enthusiastic for seeking "the meaning of living and serving, and the purpose of life" (Mahdi & Bright, 2010, p. 21) through interactive activities with students.

In Harper and Ross's (2011) experience, teaching from a perspective that assumes all college students are adults (regardless of whether they meet a formal definition of adult learner) may result in a learning situation where even traditional students become more motivated and self-directed, think maturely, make good decisions, and mold themselves to a bigger picture beyond the academic world. Teachers should demonstrate personal traits such as friendliness, humor, and humility in leading adults, and be creative in their thinking about teaching strategies and methods to meet the changing needs and interests of adults (Harper & Ross, 2011).

Conclusion

While learning theory is not a substitute for practice, if properly used, theory provides a framework from which instructors can choose teaching approaches that are most appropriate for learners and the context. Colleges today are becoming more diverse through the inclusion of a wide range of traditional and nontraditional students. Equipped with the knowledge of multiple learning theories, college instructors can develop an array of teaching strategies that have proven to impact student learning. This chapter provided a theoretical foundation upon which to build sound educational practice by exploring six major theories of learning and offering general suggestions on how these theories can be applied to college-level teaching. Grounding higher education practice in sound theory and research on human learning is essential if we are to create the high-quality teaching and learning that our colleges, universities, and society require.

References

Alexander, P. A., & Winne, P. H. (Eds.). (2006) *Handbook of educational psychology* (2nd ed.). London, UK: Lawrence Erlbaum Associates.

Bandura, A. (1986). *Social foundations of thought and action: A social cognitive theory.* Englewood Cliffs, NJ: Prentice-Hall.

Bandura, A. (2002). Social cognitive theory in cultural context. *Applied Psychology, 51*(2), 269-290.

Boeve, J. (2012). An overview of Malcolm Knowles' concepts of andragogy. *DEOracle@ UMUC.* Retrieved from http://webcache.googleusercontent.com/search?q=cache:hCFV-lJ4m4wJ:deoracle.org/online-pedagogy/teaching-strategies/an-overview-of-malcolm-knowles%27-concept-of-andragogy.html+&cd=1&hl=en&ct=clnk&gl=us&client=firefox-a

Boyd, R. D. (1991). *Personal transformations in small groups.* New York, NY: Routledge.

Boyd, R. D., & Myers, J. G. (1988). Transformative education. *International Journal of Lifelong Education, 7*(4), 261-284.

Chan, S. (2010). Applications of andragogy in multi-disciplined teaching and learning. *Journal of Adult Education, 39*(2), 25-35.

Cook, D. A. (1997). Behavioral analysis as a basis for instructional design. In C. R. Dills & A. J. Romiszowski (Eds.), *Instructional development paradigms* (pp. 215-244). Englewood Cliffs, NJ: Educational Technology Publications.

Cranton, P. (1994). *Understanding and promoting transformative learning: A guide for educators of adults.* San Francisco, CA: Jossey-Bass.

Daloz, L. (1986). *Effective teaching and mentoring: Realizing the transformational power of adult learning experiences.* San Francisco, CA: Jossey-Bass.

D'Amato, L. G., & Krasny, M. E. (2011). Outdoor adventure education: Applying transformative learning theory to understanding instrumental learning and personal growth in environmental education. *Journal of Environmental Education, 42*(4), 237-254.

Dimitriadis, G., & Kamberelis, G. (2006). *Theory for education.* New York, NY: Routledge.

Ertmer, P., & Newby, T. (1993). Behaviorism, cognitivism, constructivism: Comparing critical features from an instructional design perspective. *Performance Improvement Quarterly, 6*(4), 50-72.

Freire, P. (1984). *Pedagogy of the oppressed.* New York, NY: Continuum.

Gage, N. L., & Berliner, D. C. (1998). *Educational psychology* (6th ed.). Boston, MA: Houghton Mifflin.

Glover, J. A., & Ronning, R. R. (Eds.). (1987). *Historical foundations of educational psychology.* New York, NY: Plenum.

Goddu, K. (2012). Meeting the challenge: Teaching strategies for adult learners. *Kappa Delta Pi Record, 48,* 169-173.

Gredler, M. E. (1992). *Learning and instruction: Theory into practice.* New York, NY: Macmillan.

Harper, L., & Ross, J. (2011). An application of Knowles' theories of adult education to an undergraduate interdisciplinary studies degree program. *The Journal of Continuing Higher Education, 59,* 161-166. doi: 10.1080/07377363.2011.614887

Houle, C. O. (1996). *The design of education.* San Francisco, CA: Jossey-Bass.

Hoyt, J. E., Howell, S. L., Touchet, J., Young, S., & Wygant, S. (2010). Enhancing nontraditional student learning outcomes in higher education. *Journal of Lifelong Learning, 19,* 23-37.

Huitt, W. (2009). Humanism and open education. *Educational Psychology Interactive.* Valdosta, GA: Valdosta State University. Retrieved from http://www.edpsycinteractive.org/topics/affect/humed.html

Illeris, K. (2004). *The three dimensions of learning.* Malabar, FL: Keieger.

Imel, S. (1998). *Transformative learning in adulthood.* (ERIC Document Reproduction Services No. ED423426).

Keesee, G. S. (2010). *Andragogy: Adult learning theory.* Retrieved from http://teachinglearningresources.pbworks.com/w/page/30310516/Andragogy--Adult%20Learning%20Theory

Knowles, M. S. (1980). *The modern practice of adult education: From pedagogy to andragogy.* Englewood Cliffs, NJ: Cambridge Adult Education.

Knowles, M. S., Holton, E. G., & Swanson, R. A. (1998). *The adult learner: The definitive classic in adult education and human resources development.* Houston, TX: Gulf Publishing Company.

Koopman, G. R. (1987). The thread of humanism in the history of American education. *Journal of Curriculum and Supervision, 2*(3), 233-247.

Mahdi, G. S., & Bright, L. K. (2010). Andragogy—A mantra for US/Iraqi cross-cultural dialogue. *Journal of Adult Education, 39*(1), 18-25.

Matthews, W. J. (2003, Summer). Constructivism in the classroom: Epistemology, history, and empirical evidence [Electronic version]. *Teacher Education Quarterly,* 51-64.

Mayer, R. E. (1992). Cognition and instruction: Their historic meeting within educational psychology. *Journal of Educational Psychology, 84,* 405-412.

McGrath, V. (2009). Reviewing the evidence on how adult students learn: An examination of Knowles' model of andragogy. *Adult Learner: The Irish Journal of Adult and Community Education, 12,* 99-110.

Merriam, S. B. (2001). Andragogy and self-directed learning: Pillars of adult learning theory. *New Direction for Adult and Continuing Education, 89,* 3-91.

Merriam, S. B., & Caffarella, R. S. (1991). *Learning in adulthood: A comprehensive guide.* San Francisco, CA: Jossey-Bass.

Merriam, S. B., Caffarella, R. S., & Baumgartner, L. M. (2007). *Learning in adulthood: A comprehensive guide.* San Francisco, CA: Jossey-Bass.

Mezirow, J. (1998). On critical reflection. *Adult Education Quarterly, 48*(3), 185-198.

Ornstein, A. C., & Levine, D. U. (2008). *Foundations of education* (10th ed.). Boston, MA: Houghton Mifflin.

Pavlov, I. P. (1927). *Conditioned reflexes.* New York, NY: Dover.

Phillips, D. C., & Soltis, J. F. (2004). *Perspectives on learning* (4th ed.). New York, NY: Teaching College, Columbia University.

Pintrich, P. R., Cross, D. R., Kozma, R. B., & McKeachie, W. J. (1986). Instructional psychology. *Annual Review of Psychology, 37,* 611-651.

Ross-Gordon, J. M. (2011, Winter). Research on adult learners: Supporting the needs of a student population that is no longer nontraditional. *Peer Review, 13*(1), 26-29.

Schunk, D. H. (2000). *Learning theories: An educational perspective* (3rd. ed.).Upper Saddle River, NJ: Merrill.

Skinner, B. F. (1938). *The behavior of organisms.* New York, NY: Appleton-Century-Crofts.

Skinner, B. F. (1953). *Science and human behavior.* New York, NY: Macmillan.

Snowman, J., McCown, R., & Biehler, R. (2009). *Psychology applied to teaching* (12th ed.). Boston, MA: Houghton Mifflin.

Stevens-Long, J., Schapiro, S. A., & McClintock, C. (2012). Passionate scholars: Transformative learning in doctoral education. *Adult Education Quarterly, 62*(2), 180-198. doi: 10.1177/0741713611402046

Svinicki, M. D. (2004). *Learning and motivation in the postsecondary classroom.* Boston, MA: Anker.

Taylor, E. W. (1998). *The theory and practice of transformative learning: A critical review.* Columbus, OH: Eric Clearinghouse on Adult, Vocational and Continuing Education.

Taylor, E. W. (2008). Transformative learning theory. *New Directions for Adult and Continuing Education, 119,* 5-15.

Taylor, G. R., & MacKenney, L. (2008). *Improving human learning in the classroom:Theories and teaching practices.* Lanham, MD: Rowman & Littlefield Education.

Thorndike, E. L. (1906). *Principles of learning.* New York, NY: Seiler.

Thorndike, E. L. (1911). *Animal intelligence.* New York, NY: Macmillian.

Warrick, W. R. (2001). *Constructivism: Pre-historical to post modern.* Retrieved from George Mason University website: http://mason.gmu.edu/~wwarrick/Portfolio/Products/PDF/constructivism.pdf

Watson, J. B. (1913). Psychology as the behaviorist views it. *Psychological Bulletin, 20,* 158-177.

Watson, J. B. (1925). *Behaviorism.* New York, NY: Norton.

Wilson, B. G., & Myers, K. M. (2000). Situated cognition in theoretical and practical context. In D. H. Jonassen & S. M. Land (Eds.), *Theoretical foundations of learning environments* (pp. 57-88). Mahwah, NJ: Lawrence Erlbaum Associates.

Woolfolk, A. (2001). *Educational psychology* (8th ed.). Needham Heights, MA: Allyn and Bacon.

Zmeyov, S. I. (1998). Andragogy: Origins, developments and trends. *International Review Education, 44*(1), 103-108.

Chapter 4

Critical Pedagogy and the Struggle for Social Change

Nana Osei-Kofi

We live in a time when proponents of critical pedagogy argue for its vital importance as a response to current social, political, and economic conditions. At stake are the values of participatory democracy, the public good, civic discourse, and dissent—values that are often forcefully pushed aside in contemporary society in favor of deregulation and privatization of public systems, antidemocratic profit-generating practices, and the commodification of nearly all spheres of life. So what is critical pedagogy and why is it significant to this historical moment? In an effort to answer these questions, this chapter focuses on providing an introduction to critical pedagogy and offers examples of how educators and their students engage in what Paulo Freire, one of the most influential education philosophers of the 20th century, described as "reading the word and reading the world" (Freire & Macedo, 1987, p. ix). For Freire and for educators who embrace critical pedagogy, education is not simply about traditional notions of literacy (reading the word), rather it is about a broader conception of learning, inclusive of the ability to understand relations of power and privilege (reading the world) and acting in response to this knowledge.

That is to say, critical pedagogy is important to this historical moment because it is a philosophy of education and of society that seeks to bring about critical inquiry, learning, and engagement that can "transform inequitable, undemocratic ... oppressive institutions and social relations" (Burbules & Berk, 1999, p. 46).

Henry Giroux, the first North American scholar to use the term *critical pedagogy* in his 1983 book *Theory and Resistance in Education*, recently commented that

> While it may be in fashion to write or edit books on critical pedagogy, with rare exceptions, the authors of these books fail, on the one hand, to capture the historical moment that gave rise to what is now critical pedagogy in the United States and, on the other hand, because of a lack of a thorough understanding of history ... often reduce critical pedagogy to a methodology to be implemented. (Giroux, 2012, p. xiii)

In an effort to avoid the misconceptions about critical pedagogy that Giroux highlights, it is important to begin by emphasizing that critical pedagogy cannot be reduced to a method of teaching. Instead, it is about a social movement, a philosophy of being, and a perspective on the world that seeks to "disrupt the effects of oppressive regimes of power both in the classroom and in the larger society" (Nikolakaki, 2012, p. xii). Describing critical pedagogy at its best, Giroux (2006) has suggested that it

> is about neither training nor political indoctrination; instead, it is about a political and moral practice that provides the knowledge, skills, and social relations that enable students to expand the possibilities of what it means to be critical citizens while using their knowledge and skills to deepen and extend the possibilities of living in a substantive and inclusive democracy. (p. 31)

That is to say, to engage with critical pedagogy is a moral choice that calls on educators to make a decision about the type of society they want to live in and the type of agency they want to instill in their students as members of society (McLaren, 1998). As Wink (2005) put it, "we don't do critical pedagogy, we *live* it" (p. 120). Further, "no formula or homogenous representation exists for the universal implementation of any form of critical pedagogy" (Darder, Baltodano, & Torres, 2003, p. 10). For example, to use teaching methods that facilitate classroom interaction (something that is often associated with critical pedagogy), while positive, is not a practice that in and of itself is informed by any political project of liberation, which is what is at the heart of critical pedagogy (Aronowitz, 2012). Put slightly differently, "simply caring about students, while necessary, does not constitute a critical pedagogy" (Kincheloe, 2008, p. 9). "In fact, it is precisely ... [the absence of a singular expression of critical pedagogy] that constitutes its critical nature, and therefore its most emancipatory and democratic function" (Darder et al., 2003, p. 11).

Historical Overview of Critical Pedagogy

The scholarship on critical pedagogy in the United States emerged as a response to dominant and oppressive conditions in society and within education in the 1980s and 1990s (Giroux, 2012; Kincheloe, 2008). It is most strongly associated with the work of scholars like Henry Giroux, Peter McLaren, Donaldo Macedo, Joe Kincheloe, Shirley Steinberg, Ira Shor, and Antonia Darder. In addition to these education scholars, the work of a number of intellectuals outside the field of education, including Noam Chomsky, bell hooks, and Howard Zinn, have made important contributions to the development of critical pedagogy. Many scholars of critical pedagogy also suggest that reaching back in history to acknowledge direct linkages to critical pedagogy in the work on education by thinkers like W.E.B. Dubois and John Dewey is of importance to a broad understanding of the field (Kincheloe, 2008; Wink, 2005). Having noted this, there is no a singular historical description that can comprehensively capture the origins and development of critical pedagogy in the United States. As Kincheloe (2008) has so aptly pointed out, "all descriptions of critical pedagogy—like knowledge in general—are shaped by those who devise them and the values they hold ... many will agree with [certain descriptions] ... while others will be disappointed—and even offended—by what ... [is] included and what ... [is] left out" (p. 5-6). In an effort to craft a characterization of the emergence of critical pedagogy in the United States, Darder et al. (2003) argued that

> In many ways, it constituted a significant attempt to bring an array of divergent views and perspectives to the table, in order to invigorate the capacity of radical educators to engage critically with the impact of capitalism and gendered, racialized relations upon the lives of students from historically disenfranchised populations. (p. 2)

Despite this lack of a single historical description of the development of critical pedagogy, scholars agree that to understand the emergence of the field, it is essential to recognize the significance of Paulo Freire's work, as well as that of the

Frankfurt School and Critical Theory, on what we know as critical pedagogy today. In the development of his educational philosophy, Freire was deeply influenced by his early work with popular education and adult literacy in Brazil. Noting that education can never be neutral (it either dominates or liberates), Freire (1970) claimed that the failure to engage with the causes of oppressive social structures advances a culture of silence and maintains a status quo that is unjust. Hence, critical pedagogy is a necessary practice for educators who believe that education should be an act of freedom. Heavily influenced by Marxist thought, Freire's idea of critical pedagogy is concerned with challenging and transforming a social structure and an education system that is viewed as designed to reproduce an unequal, undemocratic society to the benefit of a small elite.

Like Freire's philosophy, critical theory, developed by a group of German neo-Marxist intellectuals commonly referred to as the Frankfurt School, is a philosophical approach to examining society premised on understanding domination and the ways in which social transformation can alleviate oppressive social conditions and achieve liberation. Reinforcing the importance of critical theory to the foundation of critical pedagogy, Giroux (1983) has suggested that the work of the Frankfurt School "demonstrates and simultaneously calls for the necessity of ongoing critique, one in which the claims of any theory must be confronted with the distinction between the world it examines and portrays, and the world as it actually exists" (p. 28).

Critiques of Critical Pedagogy

In embracing a problem-posing approach to education that draws on the aforementioned philosophical perspectives, advocates of critical pedagogy are particularly concerned with responding to oppression and the conditions of those who are marginalized in contemporary society (Kincheloe, 2008). Having said that, historically, critical pedagogy has not been without its critics when it comes to the question of responding to, and addressing, oppression. For example, although there are strong points of connection between feminist pedagogy and critical pedagogy (both are concerned with transforming the classroom, challenging oppression and domination, and struggling for equity), some of the most well-known critiques of critical pedagogy have come from feminist scholars (e.g., Gore, 1993; Lather, 1998), many of whom have argued that because critical pedagogy comes out of a patriarchal understanding of the world, it lacks awareness and attention to the ways in which sexism shapes relations of domination.

Additionally, the language of critical pedagogy has been critiqued for being inaccessible by a range of scholars who have suggested this represents elitism, as well as a contradiction, if the purpose of the work is to engage with and address oppression (Nygreen, 2010). Ethnic studies scholars and scholars of color have expressed concerns about the field of critical pedagogy as a White male domain in which women and people of color are largely absent (Allen, 2004). Furthermore, concerns about the lack of engagement with disability in critical pedagogy have been raised, with scholars noting an absence of analysis of the disabled body, and the role of disability, in unequal social and educational conditions (Erevelles, 2000; Gabel, 2002).

A strong critique from within critical pedagogy concerns discussions of a retreat from class analysis. This viewpoint suggests that scholarship on critical pedagogy has experienced a turn toward analyses of the ways in which culture reproduces inequity at the expense of a focus on economics. These critics argue that analyses of cultural politics decenter the examination of class relations as essential to understanding capitalist society, therefore, eschewing the ways in which these relations shape education (Cho, 2006). Meanwhile, others contend that a focus on culture, in concert with an emphasis on class relations and a critique of capitalism, can advance critical pedagogies' ultimate goal of achieving a more just society.

Another critique from scholars invested in the project of critical pedagogy concerns what Apple (2013) described as *romantic possibilitarianism*. He argued that too often critical pedagogy texts overemphasize a language of possibility, without being sufficiently grounded in and focused on the specifics of educational policy and practice. Moreover, he noted that the focus on possibilities often also comes at the expense of giving attention to the lived experiences of educators, students, and larger communities, thus abandoning any possibility of radical action leading to material change (Apple, 2013; McArthur, 2010).

Reflecting on the many critiques, both external and internal to critical pedagogy, McArthur (2010) has suggested that differences and disagreements among proponents of various critical and emancipatory pedagogies stand in the way of productive change through a valuing of varying perspectives and conflict. Therefore, he has argued that to realize the political aims of critical pedagogy, it is necessary for scholars to "find ways to both respect the differences that have inspired so many diverse pedagogies and to build links between these pedagogies" (McArthur, 2010, p. 498).

Practicing Critical Pedagogy

To practice critical pedagogy, at its most basic level, is to engage in a problem-posing education (Freire, 1970). That is to say, it is about (a) identifying and giving name to the problems that are in need of being addressed, (b) analyzing the causes of the problems at a root level, and (c) finding solutions for these problems. Friere called upon educators "to name, to reflect critically, [and] to act" (Wink, 2003, p. 3). For practitioners to engage deeply with critical pedagogy is to "strive ... to make transparent the complexity of the relationships between teachers and students, teaching and learning, schooling and the world-at-large. It is about shared responsibility for a possible future" (Goldstein & Beutel, 2007, p. 3). Further, Giroux and Searls Giroux (2006) argued that,

> Pedagogy as a critical practice should provide the classroom conditions that provide the knowledge, skills, and culture of questioning necessary for students to engage in critical dialogue with the past, question authority (whether sacred or secular) and its effects, struggle with ongoing relations of power, and prepare themselves for what it means to be critical, active citizens in the interrelated local, national, and global public spheres. (p. 82)

To create this type of a learning experience, dialogue is central. In practicing *problem-posing education,* not only do students learn from educators, but educators also learn from students. It is a practice that assumes that all students, as a result of their varied lived experiences, have something meaningful to contribute to the learning process. Through careful analysis and deep reflection, the aim of this type of dialogue is to foster critical consciousness in students. Freire believed that through critical consciousness (i.e., *conscientization*), students develop a deep sense of the ways in which their social conditions are shaped by the society in which they live, as well as their capacity to influence and alter these conditions. To reshape conditions through action is what Freire referred to as *praxis,* the coming together of theory and practice. Throughout this process, Freire (1998) declared that it is important to create an environment where (a) students' intellectual curiosity is sustained, (b) questioning is endless, and (c) there is a sense of the unfinished nature of coming to know. Contrasting this dialogical approach to education to dominant practices, Freire described traditional education as a banking model, where students are viewed as empty vessels into which educators deposit knowledge. This is an approach Freire claimed not only dehumanizes students but also maintains the status quo. It is important here to recognize that when Freire argued for moving away from the premise of depositing knowledge, he was not advocating educators no longer teach. Instead, he believed that teaching centers on stimulating and creating spaces and possibilities for knowledge production, rather than mechanical transfers of knowledge (Freire, 1998).

The Critical Pedagogy Classroom

Educators and others who are new to critical pedagogy will quickly discover there is significantly more theoretical work on critical pedagogy than work that explores actual classroom practices. This is not surprising since critical pedagogy is *not* a method. Additionally, as a philosophy, there is no singular way to implement critical pedagogy, especially since the ways in which it is manifest in a classroom are determined by myriad factors that are contextually and historically grounded. However, scholars have attempted to look at classrooms where critical pedagogy is practiced in an effort to identify common themes.

In a study of 17 educators committed to critical pedagogy, Breunig (2009) found the vehicles through which they actualized their practices centered on "dialogue, group work; co-construction of syllabus [sic]; and experiential activities" (p. 247). As noted earlier, while practices such as these are valuable to the student experience, they do not in and of themselves represent a practice of critical pedagogy, unless explicitly tied to a political project of social transformation. Attentive to this issue, Breunig recognized that many of her study participants might not be viewed as engaging in critical pedagogy. Rather than dismiss these practices, however, she argued that to create a classroom embodying the values of social justice can itself be thought of as a act of social justice, especially in spaces where this is counter to the dominant environment. Breunig also questioned whether what she described as the dominance of *implicit* praxis, could be called critical pedagogy, suggesting "there may be a need for critical pedagogues to continue to broaden their understandings of the justice-oriented nature of critical praxis and to begin to articulate this intent more explicitly within their postsecondary classroom practices" (p. 260).

In a more expansive study focused on students' experiences, Goomansingh (2009) found the critical pedagogy classroom was defined by a focus on (a) student voice; (b) an engagement with complex social conditions of difference, power, and privilege; and (c) the ways in which educators used their authority to establish a democratic space for critical engagement. Based on her findings, Goomansingh also suggested some of the challenges that come with attempting to practice a critical pedagogy using the aforementioned strategies include addressing the unequal participation by students in dialogue, resulting from issues of difference and power, and advancing an explicit understanding of the ways in which educator authority and freedom can co-exist in a critical classroom (i.e., authority used to ensure a democratic space rather than to squelch freedom).

Examples of Critical Pedagogy in the Classroom

This section offers examples of different ways in which university educators have worked to put critical pedagogy into practice in their classrooms. Themes that emerge from these studies are also discussed.

Ethnobotany and a Critical Pedagogy of Place

In her case study of critical pedagogical practice in an ethnobotany seminar at the University of New Mexico, Brandt (2004) described the ways in which her students engaged with "social, economic, and ecological relationships beyond the university community" (p. 93). Focusing on ecojustice and the study of the uses of plants by humans, this topic was explored through a critical theoretical perspective, affording students the opportunity to engage with questions of epistemology in relation to both Western science and traditional ecological knowledge, such as "What counts as science? Whose knowledge is valued? What knowledge can sustain … communities?" (p. 93). In addition to exploring Western scientific knowledge, students also went outside the traditional classroom to learn from members of the local community. By talking to farmers, tribal land use managers, and traditional healers in the Latino community, students learned about indigenous knowledge systems and the struggle to maintain these within local communities. Through this process of exploring both traditional Western science and local knowledge systems, students developed an understanding of the ways in which political, economic, cultural, and environmental forces shape not only what counts as scientific knowledge but also the knowledge claims of traditional science.

In addition to writing papers that critically analyzed the scientific literature, students wrote ethnobotanical autobiographies, exploring how local knowledge systems shaped their own lives—a process through which science was no longer something outside of their lives but something personal. Making meaning of her practice, Brandt (2004) argued that

> Integrating epistemology and place into the university curriculum can bring students to a new level of activism and democratic participation at the university. This approach is not intent on

> reproducing liberal ideologues, but citizens who can *think and act* [emphasis in original]: students who have the skill to evaluate "knowledge," negotiate diverse points of view, and build a consensus toward creating sustainable communities. (p. 94)

In Brandt's (2004) description of her class, key elements of critical pedagogy that were emphasized included the importance of understanding the local context and challenging the separation of local communities from the university. Additionally, she created a learning environment in which students were able to think critically about the assumptions, values, and beliefs that defined their understanding of reality and their place within the larger community. Challenging what she described as the ways in which traditional approaches to "the teaching of science reinforces a passive citizenry" (p. 94), Brandt's seminar focused on asking difficult questions about knowledge, power, inclusion, and exclusion in science. Students engaged with these questions through critical study and analysis. In her reflection on her practice, Brandt noted that using a critical pedagogy of place opens up "possibilities for students, researchers, and community members to join in understanding local contexts and indigenous knowledge systems, and to test new ways of living in our world" (p. 105).

Critical Pedagogy in a Language Foundations Course

Kadi-Hanifi's (2009) description of her language foundations course at the University of Birmingham and the practice of critical pedagogy focused on getting students to engage with the relationship of the English language to racism, classism, and imperialism. To expose students to the power and politics of language, Kadi-Hanifi introduced them to English literature by Asian and African writers as a way to raise critical issues about English as a world language, and to reflect on this through the perspectives of these writers. These readings also encouraged lively discussions about language and colonialism, the expression of non-Western realities through the English language, and how the English language in former colonies is changing to better reflect the realities of these societies. Through a panel debate exercise, students assumed different positions in relationship to English as a global language: on the one hand, in favor of English as a useful mode to express non-White realities, and on the other, in opposition to English because of its links to imperialism and racism. Kadi-Hanifi argued this approach "helps students to move away from expressing their own possibly 'biased' perspectives, as they have to concentrate on playing a role rather than exposing their true views" (p. 95). Through this process, she suggested, "learning and knowledge are ... created 'despite the views held' or without 'feeling guilty/embarrassed in the company of peers'"(p. 95).

Similar to Brandt's (2004) approach in her ethnobotany class, Kadi-Hanifi (2009) used autobiographic writing as a way to engage students with issues of bilingualism, classism, and education. Students wrote about experiences with language prejudice in the education system, such as teachers showing bias against nondominant languages and dialects. Kadi-Hanifi also used (a) role-play to engage with difficult content; (b) critical discourse analysis to explicitly connect with language and power; (c) creative writing to help students express their experience with the class; and (d) shared decision making about the course content to empower students as knowledge producers.

In her approach to teaching, Kadi-Hanifi created an environment where students were able to make connections between their own lives, the larger community, and the politics of language. Students were afforded the intellectual tools and necessary skills to critically analyze content and had opportunities throughout the class to reflect on their experiences and what they were learning. Finally, this student-centered approach challenged the banking model of education, focusing instead on creating an environment where students could come to critical consciousness.

Learning for Social Justice in a First-Year Seminar

Education for Social Justice is a course offered at the University of Wyoming and designed to introduce first-year students to social justice and social activism in education. Instructors Fuentes, Chanthongthip, and Rios (2010) described their course as one that aims to "provide an apprenticeship in teaching for social justice, including active learning in preparation for social activism" (p. 363). For example, to address bias at the individual level, students were asked to respond to a list of actual situations that had occurred in schools around the country. Like Kadi-Hanifi (2009), Fuentes and his colleagues also used role-play to stimulate discussion about how to react when faced with social injustice. In another class activity connecting questions of social justice to education, students read the 1972 Black Panther Platform and Program and, based on this model, developed plans for social justice in education, paying attention to their own sense of responsibility for fostering a democratic society.

In teaching the class, Fuentes and his co-instructors (2010) learned that using current events to expose students to injustice, "challenge[d] students to view their world as rife with social ills that require[d] their immediate attention and help[ed] them to develop tools for handling social injustices" (p. 366). Similar to

Brandt's (2004) and Kadi-Hanifi's (2009) experiences, Fuentes and his colleagues found great power in connecting the course content to students' personal experiences and commitments. This was particularly evident in the assignment based on the Black Panther Party Platform, where students were asked to create their own platform for socially just education. Noting the influence of real-life examples on developing students' critical consciousness, Fuentes and his colleagues suggested that "because so many students do not hold an image of a socially just society as a likely possibility. ... real life examples help students ... develop a vision of the future where positive social action can be successfully implemented" (p. 367).

This course and the previous examples illustrate attention to local context, a connection between micro- and macro-level social realities, the importance of action through making the connection between theory and practice (i.e., praxis), and valuing student voice. They also speak to how personal connections to course content bring material to life and facilitate a critical understanding of the significance of current social, political, and economic realities.

Conclusion

Resonating with the viewpoints introduced at the beginning of this chapter, Goomansingh (2009), in her study, warned of the impact of capitalism on education and society and argued that a practice of critical pedagogy cannot claim to work for democracy without addressing the ills of capitalism and the ways in which current social conditions are eroding any notion of higher education for the public good. She suggested that

> At the core of critical pedagogy, teachers and students must become public intellectuals who are politically engaged to address the human condition and challenge social inequities. The struggle for democracy requires education, as a public space, to develop a community of teachers and students who strive for the democratic imperative. (pp. 233-234)

To this point, Freire argued that "education is influenced by all sectors of society, but it is the only sector that can influence all sectors of society" (Nikolakaki, 2012, p. xii). This suggests that to be an educator with a belief in the need for social transformation and the possibility of a more just society, engaging with emancipatory pedagogies, such as critical pedagogy in the current historical moment, is not optional—it is an absolute necessity.

References

Allen, R. (2004). Whiteness and critical pedagogy. *Educational Philosophy and Theory, 36*(2), 121-136.

Apple, M. (2013). *Knowledge, power, and education: The collected works of Michael W. Apple.* New York, NY: Routledge.

Aronowitz, S. (2012). Paulo Freire's radical democratic humanism: The fetish method. In M. Nikolakaki (Ed.), *Critical pedagogy in the new dark ages* (pp. 257-274). New York, NY: Peter Lang.

Brandt, C. (2004). A thirst for justice in the arid Southwest: The role of epistemology and place in higher education. *Educational Studies, 36*(1), 93-107.

Breunig, M. (2009). Teaching for and about critical pedagogy in the post-secondary classroom. *Studies in Social Justice, 3*(2), 247-262.

Burbules, N., & Berk, R. (1999). Critical thinking and critical pedagogy: Relations, differences, and limits. In T. Popkewitz & L. Fendler (Eds.), *Critical theories in education: Changing terrains of knowledge and politics* (pp. 45-65). New York, NY: Routledge.

Cho, S. (2006). On language of possibility: Revisiting critical pedagogy. In C. Rossatto, R. Allen, & M. Pruyn (Eds.), *Reinventing critical pedagogy: Widening the circle of anti-oppressive education* (pp. 125-141). Lanham, MD: Rowan & Littlefield.

Darder, A., Baltodano, M., & Torres, R. (Eds.). (2003). *The critical pedagogy reader.* New York, NY: Routledge.

Erevelles, N. (2000). Educating unruly bodies: Critical pedagogy, disability studies, and the politics of schooling. *Educational Theory, 50*(1), 25-47.

Freire, P. (1970). *Pedagogy of the oppressed.* New York, NY: Seabury.

Freire, P. (1998). *Pedagogy of freedom: Ethics, democracy and civic courage.* Lanham, MD: Rowman & Littlefield.

Freire, P., & Macedo, D. P. (1987). *Literacy: Reading the word and the world.* South Hadley, MA: Bergin Garvey.

Fuentes, R., Chanthongthip, L., & Rios, F. (2010). Teaching and learning social justice as an "intellectual community" requirement: Pedagogical opportunities and student understandings. *Equity & Excellence in Education, 43*(3), 357-374.

Gabel, S. (2002). Some conceptual problems with critical pedagogy. *Curriculum Inquiry, 32*(2), 177-201.

Giroux, H. (1983). *Theory and resistance in education.* South Hadley, MA: Bergin & Garvey.

Giroux, H. (2006). Academic freedom under fire: The case for critical pedagogy. *College Literature, 33*(4), 1-42.

Giroux, H. (2012). Rethinking the promise of critical pedagogy: A foreword. In M. Nikolakaki (Ed.), *Critical pedagogy in the new dark ages* (pp. xiii-xvii). New York, NY: Peter Lang.

Giroux, H., & Searls Giroux, S. (2006). Challenging neoliberalism's new world order: The promise of critical pedagogy. *Cultural Studies-Critical Methodologies, 6*(21), 21-32.

Goldstein, R., & Beutel, A. (2007). Introduction: Why a book on "useful theory"? What makes theory "useful"? In Goldstein, R. (Ed.), *Useful theory: Making critical education practical* (pp. 1-11). New York, NY: Peter Lang.

Goomansingh, R. (2009). *Using critical pedagogy to educate for democracy in the graduate classroom* (Doctoral dissertation). University of Toronto, Ontario, Canada.

Gore, J. (1993). *The struggle for pedagogies.* New York, NY: Routledge.

Kadi-Hanifi, K. (2009). Using critical pedagogies from adult education to inspire and challenge higher education students. *Learning and Teaching, 2*(1), 80-103.

Kincheloe, J. (2008). *Critical pedagogy primer.* New York, NY: Peter Lang.

Lather, P. (1998). Critical pedagogy and its complicities: A praxis of stuck places. *Educational Theory, 48*(4), 487-497.

McArthur, J. (2010). Achieving social justice within and through higher education: The challenge for critical pedagogy. *Teaching in Higher Education, 15*(5), 493-504.

McLaren, P. (1998). Revolutionary pedagogy in post-revolutionary times: Rethinking the political education. *Educational Theory, 48*(4), 431-462.

Nikolakaki, M. (Ed.). (2012). *Critical pedagogy in the new dark ages.* New York, NY: Peter Lang.

Nygreen, K. (2010). The central paradox of critical pedagogy: Learning from practice in an urban 'last chance' high school. In L. Schreff & K. Spector (Eds.), *Culturally relevant pedagogy: Clashes and confrontations* (pp. 61-87). Lanham, MD: Rowman & Littlefield.

Wink, J. (2005). *Critical pedagogy: Notes from the real world.* Boston, MA: Pearson.

Chapter 5
Embracing Contemplative Pedagogy in a Culturally Diverse Classroom

Laura I. Rendón and Vijay Kanagala

With researchers (e.g., Shapiro, Brown, & Astin, 2011) substantiating the beneficial effects of meditation and other contemplative practices in educational settings, advocates and practitioners of contemplative pedagogy have proposed integrating these approaches into the curriculum to help learners reach the highest standards of what it means to be educated in a complex, ever-changing world. Through contemplative processes, a deep, holistic learning experience can be generated that activates and deepens an individual's outer learning outcomes, such as critical thinking, information processing, and academic achievement. Inner awareness can also be fostered, including developing a sense of purpose, concentration, and presence; enhancing psychological well-being; becoming creative; developing self-compassion; and building positive interpersonal relationships (Rendón, 2009; Shapiro, Brown, & Astin, 2011).

A key aspect of contemplative pedagogy is the notion that a cutting-edge and integrative, even revolutionary, education can be advanced when energies and resources are intentionally devoted to educating the whole student. This happens when social, emotional, and spiritual development, together with academic achievement, are intertwined (indeed, become interdependent) to engage the full complexity of the learner's cognitive and intuitive skills. In short, both inner and outer engagement are critical to create the highest standards of educational excellence. This chapter focuses on providing background information about contemplative pedagogy and offers examples of how to employ contemplative practices in culturally diverse classrooms while attending to contemporary social justice issues.

History of Contemplative Education and Holistic Approaches

Traditional and contemporary Western models of education have largely focused on privileging certain forms of teaching and learning. For example, publishing, speaking engagements, and writing grants are typically acknowledged as the best scholarly practices while best classroom pedagogy tends to favor teaching or lecturing, curriculum development, and working with students. These practices (or outer engagement) are most familiar to us because of the constant reinforcement and validation that we receive for them throughout our lives and educational journeys. They are usually associated with the mind and influence our intellectualism, rationality, and objectivity. On the other hand, inner engagement relates to one's own being and offers a deeper sense of purpose and meaning in the learning process. Unlike outer engagement, it embraces subjectivity, intuition, emotion, and personal experiences. Educators are often trained to remove or distance the inner engagement in our education systems. This imbalance between the outer and inner engagements, and privileging one way of knowing over the other, have often invalidated or dismissed the ways of knowing of Indigenous populations and people of color.

To illuminate this imbalance, Lorde (1984) stated, "The white fathers told us: I think, therefore I am. The Black mother within each of us—the poet—whispers in our dreams: I feel, therefore I can be free" (p. 38). What she is expressing goes beyond the stereotyped White rational male contrasted with the emotional Black female. Rather, Lorde is implying that both feeling and thinking are important and our inner and outer processes are there for a reason, giving us choices and combinations with which to express ourselves and engage in learning experiences. Everyone possesses the ability to be rational and emotional; however, dominant social forces can often focus on rationality as the highest and perhaps only way to develop as human beings.

The epistemological view that the world order and human processes should nurture both the inner and outer person is rooted in Indigenous wisdom. However, over time, the academy has moved away from acknowledging the interconnected aspects of human development to separating and disconnecting alternative ways of engaging with the world (Rendón, 2009). Ancestral ways of knowing were based on wholeness and the unity of existence. Faith and reason, as well as science and the divine, were not separate but viewed as two parts of one whole (Palmer, 2007). Native people have their own notions of education. For example, Cajete (2000) pointed out there is no word for education in most Indigenous languages. Rather, education is best described as "coming to know" (p. 69), which entails a journey, a process, a questioning for knowledge and understanding. A visionary tradition adds understandings that, among other things, encompass harmony, compassion, hunting, planting, cycle, balance, death, and renewal.

In the United States, the role of the teacher has not changed significantly for more than 300 years. Much of today's classroom teaching retains some of the features of the colonial model of education that existed between 1600 and 1800, which was designed for young men from elite social backgrounds. The key features of the colonial model included defining the role of the instructor as an expert in charge of everything that took place in the classroom: course content, assignments, assessment methods, and instructional strategies. Students were passive recipients of information and memorized facts. By the 19th century, higher education began to serve a broader range of students, and intellectual development and scholarly endeavors (rather than memorization) were emphasized, with increased use of lectures, demonstrations, and laboratory methods. Later, as the space race ensued, greater attention was given to science and technology. The Vietnam War gave rise to an interest in a curriculum that had relevance, meaning, and preparation for the world of work as higher education became more concerned with responsibility to the community (Fuhrmann & Grasha, 1983).

During the latter part of the 20th century, critical educators, such as Paulo Freire, Peter McLaren, bell hooks, Antonia Darder, Rodolofo Torres, Martha Baltodano, Henry Giroux, Zeus Leonardo, Ira Shor, Michael Apple, and Christine Sleeter, among others, worked with the philosophical underpinnings of critical pedagogy. (See Chapter 4 for more on critical pedagogy.) This pedagogic camp advocated that individuals should be prepared to think critically about their educational experiences and be provided with tools to (a) engage in self-empowerment, (b) strengthen democracy, and (c) become involved in social transformation. A liberating education could be achieved as students became more aware of their lived experiences and social contexts, thus developing what Freire (1971) called a *critical consciousness*—the power and ability to recognize oppression and social inequalities and to take action to remediate them. Along these lines, some scholars also began to challenge epistemological frameworks focused exclusively on rational knowing; objectivity; the divide between theory and practice; and the exclusion of the contributions of women, Indigenous people, and scholars of color (Dei, Hall, & Rosenberg, 2000; Gilligan, 1982; Grande, 2004; Lather, 1991; Latina Feminist Group, 2001; Osei-Kofi, Richards, & Smith, 2004; Tuhiwai Smith, 1999).

In the late 1980s and 1990s, the concepts of *connected teaching* (Belenky, Clinchy, Goldberger, & Tarule, 1986), *engaged pedagogy* (hooks, 1994), and *holistic education* (Miller, 1997) began to emerge with a focus on a pedagogy that emphasized the union of mind, body, and spirit; the inner life of students and teachers; the connection between learning in the classroom and life experiences; and the empowerment of both teachers and students. Organizations such as the Collaborative for Academic, Social, and Emotional Learning (CASEL) advanced the benefits of social and emotional learning, associating it with promoting positive student behaviors while developing improvements in academic performance and attitudes toward school, as well as preparing young people for adulthood. The Center for Contemplative Mind in Society partnered with the American Council of Learned Societies in offering fellowships for courses that integrated contemplative practice into faculty teaching methods or content resulting in more than 150 fellows in 100 colleges and universities throughout the nation (Center for Contemplative Mind in Society, n.d.-a).

During this same period, meditation, yoga, and other contemplative practices became the subject of hundreds of studies that demonstrated their physical and mental benefits conducted by institutions such as the Brain Imaging Laboratory at the University of Wisconsin, MIT, Yale, and Harvard Medical School (Center for Contemplative Mind in Society, n.d.-c). In addition, the Center for Contemplative Mind created a Tree of Contemplative Practices (Figure 5.1) to illustrate the diverse array of stillness, generative, creative, activist, relational, movement, and ritual or cyclical practices that individuals might employ. These practices are represented by the branches in the contemplative tree. For example, by engaging in stillness practices, one can practice quieting the mind and body to develop calmness and focus. Stillness practices may include meditation, silence, centering, and quieting the mind. Similarly, relational practices emerge as powerful sources of contemplation when a group of individuals relate to one another by engaging in respectful interactions that connect their hearts and minds. Deep listening, which entails being fully present not controlling or judging what is happening in the moment, or by creating a Council Circle, a Native American tradition of engaging in dialogue, are a few ways of engaging in relational practices.

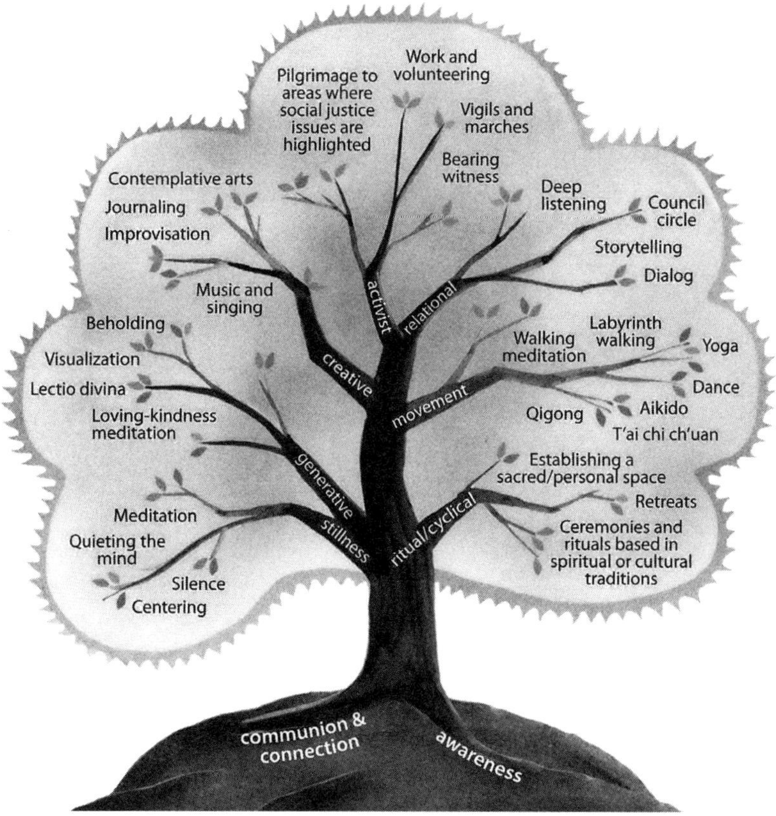

Figure 5.1. Tree of contemplative practices. Adapted from "*The Tree of Contemplative Practices*," The Center for Contemplative Mind in Society website (Center for Contemplative Mind in Society, n.d.-b). Copyright 2000-2014 by The Center for Contemplative Mind in Society. Reprinted with permission.

Especially during the latter part of the 1990s and early 2000s, models such as integrative learning and transdisciplinary education began to receive significant attention. Integrative learning was described in at least two ways. The American Association of Colleges and Universities (AAC&U) and the Carnegie Foundation for the Advancement of Teaching issued a 2004 position statement (as cited in Huber & Hutchings, 2005) explaining that integrative learning reached "across courses, over time, and between campus and community life"(p. 13). Integrative learning was proposed as connecting skills and knowledge from multiple sources and experiences, applying theory to practice, using diverse and even contradictory points of view, and understanding issues and positions contextually. Knowledge came from diverse disciplines, and learning was stretched to go beyond academic boundaries. Another approach, put forward by various organizations, such as the Fetzer Institute, Naropa University, and the California Institute for Integral Studies, promoted integrative learning as a way of addressing the whole human being—mind, body, and spirit—as well as integrating the outer life of vocation and professional responsibility and the inner life of personal development, meaning, and purpose.

Transdisciplinary studies build on interdisciplinary, multidisciplinary, and integrative models, yet emphasize a learning approach across, between, beyond, and outside all disciplines (McGregor, 2004). The key aspects of a transdisciplinary education include collaboration, problem solving, real-world engagement, openness to all disciplines, rigor, and tolerance (International Center for Transdisciplinary Research, 1994; McGregor, 2004).

Organizations and institutions, such as the Center for Contemplative Mind in Society; the Garrison Institute; Collaborative for Academic, Social, and Emotional Learning (CASEL); Naropa University; the California Institute of Integral Studies; the Mind and Life Institute; and AAC&U, have advanced the working knowledge and importance of meditation, mindfulness, social and emotional learning skills, student competence in the area of personal and social responsibility, neuroscientific understandings of the mind, and the benefits of contemplative practice. K-16 teachers, as well as advocates of learning communities and service-learning, now often embrace the tenets of contemplative pedagogy. For example, Naropa University offers undergraduate and graduate curriculum that blends ancient Eastern educational philosophies with rigorous liberal arts training and with disciplined training of the heart. In doing so, it seeks to educate the whole person. Clearly, there are now enough developments to suggest that contemplative pedagogy is not a fad or add-on pedagogic tool. Rather, contemplative pedagogy is an essential method needed to advance the kind of teaching and learning that can ultimately transform higher education and the students it serves. It is important to remember that contemplative practice need not be disassociated from academic undertakings. Rendón (2009) posed that education should be concerned with both the *sentir* (sensing processes) of intuition and the inner life and the *pensar* (thinking processes) of intellectual pursuits. Accordingly, a *sentipensante* approach incorporates both contemplative and intellectual teaching and learning activities.

Contemplative Pedagogy in Culturally Diverse Classrooms

The emerging field of contemplative education has not addressed, for the most part, pedagogic issues related to working with a culturally diverse student body, which is a reality in many colleges and universities today. Neither do we know enough about how contemplative approaches can be employed to examine diversity and social justice issues. Consequently, there is a need to create a new *contemplative pedagogic imaginary* (i.e., an imagined vision) that embraces cultural diversity and social justice. A pedagogic imaginary is needed to engage in sensitive and reflective critical dialogues while creating spaces for students to enter conversations with a sense of openness and trust that is complemented with mutual respect, understanding, willingness to learn, care, and concern.

It is useful to note that contemplative education is not only for privileged students who attend elite, high-cost colleges and universities. The benefits of contemplative approaches should extend to first-generation students (first-gens)—those whose parents did not receive education beyond a high school diploma and who now comprise roughly 50% of the college student population (Lynch, 2013). National Center for Education Statistics data from 2010 showed the demographic breakdown of first-gens was 48.5% Latinos, 45% Black or African-American, 35% Native American, 32% Asian, and 28% White (Lynch, 2013). Further, according to Ramsey and Peale (2010),

> Roughly 30% of entering freshmen in the USA are first-generation college students, and 24%—4.5 million—are both first-gens and low income. Nationally, 89% of low-income first-gens leave college within six years without a degree. More than a quarter leave after their first year—four times the dropout rate of higher-income second-generation students. (para. 6)

Students leave for numerous reasons, including financial hardship, lack of sense of belonging, academic underpreparedness, and cultural shock, among others. Many of these students are concentrated in community colleges, Historically Black Colleges and Universities (HBCUs), and Hispanic-Serving Institutions (HSIs). The education of these students has become an important unresolved social justice issue in higher education.

In institutions with large numbers of low-income first-gens, faculty struggle with how to design a teaching and learning experience for students who

- have been oppressed, victimized, and/or marginalized;
- do not have a stable home environment;
- were invalidated (e.g., told they were stupid, lazy, or not good enough for college; not supported in their goals);
- were treated as *the other* (e.g., exoticized, viewed as different or not worthwhile); and
- had difficulties engaging in a higher education context in stark contrast to their home realities.

Consequently, a new contemplative pedagogic imaginary must attend to educating students who lack social and economic privilege in American society. Research studies (Belenky et al., 1986; Rendón, 2009; Weaver & Wilding, 2013) have substantiated that students value teaching and learning experiences where they

- find deeper meaning in what is being learned in and out of the classroom;
- gain insight;
- release pain;
- find voice;
- heal;
- come to terms with anger and shadows of life (e.g., the experience of growing up poor, absent parents, violence in home, drug and alcohol abuse, and/or depression);
- connect with others and develop new relationships;
- express love, joy, passion, and compassion;
- develop resiliency;
- engage with culturally relevant practices; and
- cultivate civic awareness along with personal and social responsibility.

What a contemplative approach might look like in culturally diverse classrooms is described below. For each example, the social justice issue being addressed is highlighted followed by models of contemplative practice.

Social Justice Issue: Transforming Low-Income Students Into Proficient Writers

In courses that enroll large numbers of low-income students, a key social justice issue is how to turn these students into proficient writers who can express themselves employing college-level writing skills. Writing is one of the most challenging skills a low-income student should master. Intellectual engagement might be fostered through traditional mechanisms, such as writing essays and poems, book reports, and research narratives. However, it is important to remember that writing can come alive when students are allowed to express themselves by reflecting on their own lived experiences.

Contemplative Practice: Poetry

The Chicago Youth Poetry Festival, the world's largest youth poetry slam, describes itself as

> A friendly competition that emphasizes self-expression and community via poetry, oral storytelling, and hip-hop spoken word, ... —a bridge—for young people from all neighborhoods, socio economic statuses, race and culture to come together and better understand one another. (Chicago Public Media, 2013, para. 1)

Understanding one's self and others through the contemplative tool of poetry has powerful lessons for the academic community. In the documentary based on the festival, *Louder Than a Bomb* (Siskel & Jacobs, 2011), one can witness the profound impact of poetry writing on students who grew up in poor neighborhoods and suffered the effects of social neglect. This was demonstrated in the film by student Nova Venerable's reading of her poem, "Apartment on Austin," about her now-absent father and her recollection of their life in an apartment where, as a nine-year old, she used her fingers to make drinks—four finger sangria, two gin, two tonic, and one lemon juice. The poem, while painful and raw, masterfully depicts life in the inner city, a reality that most Americans do not understand and will never experience. English teachers can employ slam poetry as a contemplative method to engage students in a participatory epistemology, "the knowing that occurs when the perceiver and the perceived are united as a single consciousness" (Lachman, 1998, p. 8).

Contemplative Practice: Cultural Autobiography

At the University of Texas-San Antonio, an HSI with about a 46% Latino population, students in Norma E. Cantú's English classes used photographs as a contemplative, guided imagery tool to stir imagination and write autobiographical essays based on family photographs (Rendón, 2009). Cantú herself had employed photographs of her childhood to write an autobioethnographic novel called *Canicula: Snapshots of a Girlhood en la Frontera* (Cantú, 1997). The photos became guided imagery exercises that assisted students to write from a place that honored their voice and personal experiences (Rendón, 2009).

Similarly, Puente (Bridge) Project students (typically, low-income first-gens often wounded by invalidating actions from others) in Barbara Jaffe's English class at El Camino College were encouraged to write about what they knew best—their own personal experiences (Rendón, 2009). For example, in one assignment, students wrote about their names—how they received them and their importance—and shared their work in writing *familias* (i.e., small groups). Jaffe employed an asset-based framework recognizing students' "funds of knowledge" (Moll, Amanti, Neff, & Gonzalez, 1992, p. 132) and their "community cultural wealth" (Yosso, 2005, p. 69). In other words, students were treated as competent learners who were capable of both consuming and creating knowledge and whose cultural wealth (i.e., aspirational, linguistic, familial, social, navigational, and resistant) and resiliency could be recognized and worked with in an effort to foster student success (Rendón, 2009).

Both of these examples illustrate a unique kind of pedagogy that takes students from their self-doubts to a heightened awareness about their academic abilities and future potential. In addition, they demonstrate a form of participatory epistemology that connects students to the learning experience, eliciting greater awareness about the subject matter and about themselves as learners and as human beings.

Social Justice Issue: Fostering Students' Critical Consciousness

Not all learning takes place within the confines of the classroom. Some professors engage students in service-learning activities. The National Service-Learning Clearinghouse (as cited in Guilfoile & Ryan, 2013) defines this pedagogy as, "A teaching and learning strategy that integrates meaningful community service with instruction and reflection to enrich the learning experience, teach civic responsibility, and strengthen communities" (p. 6). Because of its emphasis on reflective processes, volunteerism, and social and personal responsibility, service-learning can be employed in almost any course to actively engage students in meaningful social justice activities, such as environmental issues dealing with water quality and pollution or public concerns about the quality of education in inner city schools, to name just a few examples.

Engaging in community service-learning allows students to participate in transformative experiences that promote civic responsibility while enriching the overall learning experience. Ultimately, what can be fostered is critical consciousness, the ability to recognize inequities and take action to remediate them (Freire, 1971).

Contemplative Practice: Community Service-Learning

In Carlos Silveira's Cross-Cultural Perspectives in Art Education course at California State University-Long Beach, students learned that art is not something you just hang on a wall. Students were required to do 15 hours of service-learning with nonprofit organizations and social service agencies in Long Beach communities. For example, students worked with the Being Alive organization where they used art to help HIV positive kids and families interact better at home. Students also helped children from homeless families living in a shelter create art projects. In addition, class participants collaborated with the Latino community to create a Day of the Dead event that featured altars, dancers, and storytellers (Rendón, 2009).

Through community service-learning, Silveira employed a participatory epistemology, actively involving students in art projects within their communities to foster student development and social change. He engaged students by having them participate in activist projects that extended beyond the classroom and into the social worlds of the community. The community became a base for taking student learning to a higher level, and activist practice served to awaken a critical consciousness as students became aware of social injustices while focusing on healing and social change.

In this sense, what Freire (1971) proposed as *praxis* (i.e., action, reflection, action) became an essential process for learning. This sophisticated level of engagement transcends how student involvement is typically defined, such as meeting with faculty on a consistent basis, taking advantage of services on campus, and joining clubs or organizations (Astin, 1985). Silveira employed community service as a pedagogy to connect his students with social issues in their communities. The objective was not only to engage students in learning but also to assist students in seeing hope and possibility and becoming compassionate humanitarians.

Social Justice Issue: Exploring Social, Economic, and Cultural Inequities

American history is infused with social justice themes. From the history of violence and terrorism to the Civil Rights Movement to the heated controversies involved in conversations about race in America to how racism impacts the criminal justice system, students can engage these difficult dialogues with carefully planned intellectual and contemplative activities.

Contemplative Practice: Storytelling, Photos, and Music

Students in J. Herman Blake's African American history course at Iowa State University were required to read 16 books, write 13 papers, and meet high standards of excellence during the semester. However, they were engaged in more than academic work; students were also exposed to contemplative tools, such as storytelling, photographs, and music, to connect them with the material at deeper levels. One activity, incorporating multimodal and multisensory stimuli to create a holistic learning experience, involved students listening to an interview of a woman who was the 15th child in a family whose mother's job was to have babies. While students listened to the audio and followed the transcripts, they were provided with a visual of the woman (a photo) and had the spiritual "How Come Me Here; I Wish I Never Was Born"—selected to highlight key points in the story—play in the background (Rendón, 2009).

When addressing terrorism and violence, Blake complemented his lectures with slides from the book *Without Sanctuary* (Allen, 2000), a collection of 145 chilling photographs of lynchings in America, paired with Nina Simone singing "Strange Fruit." The strange fruit in the song referred to bodies of African Americans hanged during a lynching. Students commented that this activity was one of the most powerful experiences in class. One student said that the experience motivated him to be a humanitarian and try to change the world. Another said, "It just hurt me and made me want to do something to better my life" (Rendón, 2009, p. 129).

Contemplative Pedagogic Imaginary Embracing Cultural Diversity and Social Justice

To engage in a social-justice focused model that interconnects intellectual development with contemplative practices is exciting, yet challenging. This requires background preparation on the part of the instructor, as well as careful and sensitive development of pedagogic activities that attend to both inner and outer student engagement, while fostering high standards of educational excellence.

Background Preparation

Faculty should not engage in contemplative pedagogy without significant preparation. This involves

- ***Strong philosophical orientation about teaching and learning connected to social justice issues.*** All faculty, whether they recognize it or not, are called to deal with epistemological issues, such as: What knowledge is valued in the classroom? Who can create knowledge? and What should be a part of the curriculum? Accordingly, faculty need to be critically conscious of their own belief system and understand the implications of what it means to teach with a social justice orientation. Background knowledge can include critical pedagogy, anti-oppressive education, holistic education, and Indigenous knowledge, among others.
- ***Keen awareness of issues related to culturally diverse students, especially those who are low income and first-generation***. All too often, these students are perceived as risky college material with little to offer. This deficit-based paradigm must be replaced by an asset-based perspective that acknowledges and values these students' cultural backgrounds, and views their life experiences as important assets (Yosso,2005).
- ***Personal contemplative practice***. Kanagala and Rendón (2013) stressed that holistic classroom approaches require careful and sustained faculty development that includes background reading on the uses, potential, and challenges of employing contemplative approaches. They also emphasized the importance of faculty adopting some form of contemplative practice in their own personal lives, such as meditation, yoga, prayer, journaling, or poetry writing, among others. A personal practice allows faculty to enter the teaching and learning experience with authenticity, self-awareness, insight, and compassion. Overall, the use of contemplative approaches should be undertaken with great care and sensitivity. If poorly applied, reflective assignments can result in a less-than-positive classroom experience for instructors and students.
- ***Professional development in the uses of contemplative practice in the classroom.*** Strong preparation and professional development are needed

to guide faculty in their own personal practice and in designing courses and a classroom context that invites reflective practices. This is deep, challenging work that can, at times, lead to unexpected classroom consequences. It is safe to say that, in most instances, students will respond quite positively, but in some cases, students may exhibit negative reactions given their value system, socialization, and religious beliefs.

Preparation can assist faculty to attend to the following student outcomes:

- **inner-life competencies**, such as self-awareness, humility, authenticity, empathy, knowing one's shadow (i.e., negative aspects of ourselves we tend to ignore or downplay), building inner strength, and becoming compassionate;
- **critical consciousness**, including insight, empathy, compassion, and knowledge of the history of oppressed people and social inequities in the nation and the world;
- **awareness and appreciation of diverse ways of knowing** as demonstrated by an openness to multiple perspectives different from one's own; inclusivity; and knowledge of the intellectual contributions of diverse scholars and practitioners (e.g., women, people of color, Indigenous people, LGBT researchers); and
- **moving beyond self-awareness to social change** by using these insights to act justly and compassionately in service to the world and humanity's greater good.

Conclusion

A newly fashioned imaginary of teaching and learning for diversity and social justice requires that faculty rethink the way they teach, select content material and classroom learning activities, engage with students, and foster reflective processes. This critical task has enormous potential and carries both risks and rewards. Rendón (2009) recognized those who were willing to engage in this challenge as *spiritual warriors* on a journey to transform education. Rendón's message remains appropriate today: "May our collective breath be the vision of a transformative dream of education that speaks the language of heart and mind and the truth of wholeness, harmony, social justice, and liberation" (p. 151). Her (our) dream lives on.

References

Allen, J. (Ed.). (2000). *Without sanctuary: Lynching photography in America*. Santa Fe, NM: Twin Palms.

Astin, A. (1985). Involvement: The cornerstone for excellence. *Change, 17*(4), 35-39.

Belenky, M. F., Clinchy, B. M., Goldberger, N. R., & Tarule, J. M. (1986). *Women's ways of knowing*. New York, NY: Basics Books.

Cajete, G. A. (2000). *Native science*. Santa Fe, NM: Clear Light Publishers.

Cantú, N. (1997). *Canicula: Snapshots of a girlhood en la frontera*. Boston, MA: Houghton Mifflin.

Center for Contemplative Mind in Society. (n.d-a). *History*. Retrieved from: http://www.contemplativemind.org/programs/acmhe

Center for Contemplative Mind in Society. (n.d.- b). *The tree of contemplative practices*. Retrieved from: http://www.contemplativemind.org/practices/tree

Center for Contemplative Mind in Society. (n.d.- c). *What are contemplative practices?* Retrieved from: http://www.contemplativemind.org/practices

Chicago Public Media. (2013). *WBEZ91.5 events: Louder than a bomb 2013: The 13th annual Chicago youth poetry festival*. Retrieved October 9, 2013 from http://www.wbez.org/louder-bomb-2013-13th-annual-chicago-youth-poetry-festival-105037

Dei, G. J. S., Hall, B. L., & Rosenberg, D. G. (2000). *Indigenous knowledges in global contexts: Multiple readings of our world*. Toronto, Canada: University of Toronto Press.

Freire, P. (1971). *Pedagogy of the oppressed* (M.B. Ramos, Trans.). New York, NY: Continuum.

Fuhrmann, B. S., & Grasha, A. F. (1983). The past, present, and future in college teaching: Where does your teaching fit? In B. S. Fuhrmann & A. F. Grasha, *A practical handbook for college teachers*. Boston, MA: Little Brown & Company.

Gilligan, C. (1982). *In a different voice*. Cambridge, MA: Harvard University Press.

Grande, S. (2004). *Red pedagogy*. New York, NY: Rowman and Littlefield.

Guilfoile, L., & Ryan, M. (2013). *Linking service-learning and the common core standards: Alignment, progress, and obstacles*. Retrieved from http://gsn-newdemo2.s3.amazonaws.com/documents/1114/original/SL_and_CCSS.pdf?1392824847

hooks, b. (1994). *Teaching to transgress: Education as the practice of freedom*. New York, NY: Routledge.

Huber, M. T., & Hutchings, P. (2005). *Integrative learning: Mapping the terrain*. Washington, DC: American Association of Colleges and Universities & Carnegie Foundation for the Advancement of Teaching.

International Center for Transdisciplinary Research. (1994). *Charter of transdisciplinarity*. Retrieved from http://ciret-transdisciplinarity.org/chart.php#en

Kanagala, V., & Rendón, L. I. (2013, Summer, special issue). Birthing internal images: Employing the Cajita project as a contemplative activity in a college classroom. *New Directions for Teaching and Learning, 134*, 41-51.

Lachman, G. (1998). The archaeology of consciousness: An interview with Owen Barfield. In H. Palmer (Ed.), *Inner knowing: Consciousness, creativity, insight and intuition* (pp. 8-13). New York, NY: J. P. Tarcher/Putnam.

Lather, P. (1991). *Getting smart: Feminist research and pedagogy with/in the postmodern.* New York, NY: Routledge.

Latina Feminist Group. (2001). *Telling to live. Latina feminist testimonios.* Durham, NC: Duke University Press.

Lorde, A. (1984). *Sister outsider: Essays and speeches.* Berkeley, CA: Crossing Press.

Lynch, M. (2013). *It's tough to trailblaze: Challenges of first-generation college students.* Retrieved from: http://diverseeducation.com/article/50898/

McGregor, S. L. T. (2004). *The nature of transdisciplinary research and practice.* Retrieved from http://www.kon.org/hswp/archive/transdiscipl.pdf

Miller, R. (1997). *What are schools for? Holistic education in American culture.* Brandon, VT: Holistic Education.

Moll, L., Amanti, C., Neff, D., & Gonzalez, N. (1992). Funds of knowledge for teaching: Using a qualitative approach to connect homes and classrooms. *Theory Into Practice, 31*(2), 132-141.

Osei-Kofi, N., Richards, S., & Smith, D. (2004). Inclusion, reflection, and the politics of knowledge, (pp. 55-66). In L. I. Rendón, M. García, & D. Person (Eds.), *Transforming the first-year of college for students of color* (Monograph No. 38, pp. 55-66). Columbia, SC: University of South Carolina, National Resource Center for The First-Year Experience and Students in Transition.

Palmer, P. (2007). *The courage to teach: Exploring the inner landscape of a teacher's life.* San Francisco, CA: Jossey-Bass.

Ramsey, K., & Peale, C. (2010). *First-generation college students stay the course.* Retrieved from http://usatoday30.usatoday.com/news/education/2010-0330FirstGenDorm30_ST_N.htm

Rendón, L. I. (2009). *Sentipensante (sensing/thinking) pedagogy: Educating for wholeness, social justice and liberation.* Sterling, VA: Stylus Press.

Shapiro, S. L., Brown, K. W., & Astin, J. A. (2011). Toward the integration of meditation into higher education: A review of research evidence. *Teachers College Record, 113,* 493-528.

Siskel, J., & Jacobs, G. (Producers). (2011). *Louder than a bomb* (Movie documentary). United States: Siskel/Jacobs Productions.

Tuhiwai Smith, L. (1999). *Decolonizing methodologies.* London, UK, & New York, NY: Zed Books.

Weaver, L., & Wilding, M. (2013). *The 5 dimensions of engaged teaching: A practical guide for educators.* Bloomington, IN: Solution Tree Press.

Yosso, T. J. (2005). Whose culture has capital? A critical race theory discussion of community cultural wealth. *Race Ethnicity and Education, 8*(1), 69-91.

Chapter 6
Strengths-Oriented Teaching: Pathways to Engaged Learning

Laurie A. Schreiner

Motivating students to learn continues to be one of the major challenges facing college and university instructors today (Perry, Hall, & Ruthig, 2005; Pintrich & Zusho, 2002; Schreiner, Hulme, Hetzel, & Lopez, 2009). As a wider variety of prior learning experiences, as well as greater diversity in cultural backgrounds and learning styles, characterizes the classroom environment, engaging all students in the learning process can seem a daunting task. Strengths-oriented teaching directly addresses student motivation as its primary target, providing instructors with both a philosophy to guide their teaching as well as specific strategies for engaging students in their own learning.

Strengths-oriented teaching begins with the basic premise that students will be more motivated to invest effort in learning when they are operating from a foundation of personal assets they bring to the learning environment. Rather than focusing primarily on students' deficits—all the ways in which they are underprepared for college, for instance—a strengths-oriented approach initially focuses on the talents that students already have and then teaches them to build on those talents to address areas of challenge. Strengths-oriented pedagogy capitalizes on the instructor's strengths as well, enabling the instructor to facilitate student learning in a way that is congruent with his or her own teaching talents. In a strengths-oriented classroom, the content of the course does not change, but the instructor's approach to the students changes dramatically (Anderson, Cantwell, & Schreiner, 2004).

This approach represents a significant paradigm shift in higher education. Typically, students' deficits are the primary focus, particularly at entrance to college. In an effort to help students succeed, many colleges and universities assess students' abilities and skills at orientation and then place them in the appropriate level of coursework in order to remediate any deficits. Yet, a brief look at schedules that are full of remedial coursework leaves little doubt as to why students may appear unmotivated: Spending most of one's time in areas where one feels least competent is rarely a recipe for enthusiasm!

In this chapter, the basic components of strengths-oriented teaching will be outlined within a theoretical framework of engaged learning, motivation theory, and strengths development. Specific strengths-oriented teaching practices will be described, with examples provided for introductory-level courses as well as more advanced courses.

Engaged Learning

The primary purpose of strengths-oriented teaching is to enhance *engaged learning*, defined as "a positive energy invested in one's own learning, evidenced by meaningful processing, attention to what is happening in the moment, and involvement in learning activities" (Schreiner & Louis, 2011, p. 6). Engaged learners not only actively participate in the learning process but are also mindful and focused while learning. More importantly, engaged learners are deep learners, exhibiting a psychological engagement in the learning process characterized by meaningful processing and a focus on how their learning connects to other aspects of their lives. Such deep learning is focused on meaning-making and application, in contrast to surface learning that emphasizes rote memorization in order to pass a test (Biggs, 2003; Tagg, 2003).

Engaged learning is the desired outcome of strengths-oriented teaching practices. The goal is not only for students to be fully engaged and motivated in learning but also for their learning to last beyond the final exam. Thus, many of the strategies of strengths-oriented teaching focus specifically on students' levels of engagement and motivation in and out of the classroom.

Motivation as the Key

At the heart of engaged learning is an energy and motivation to learn that is too often missing in students—even students who are academically successful. When the motivation is missing, learning tends to remain at a surface level, remembering facts long enough to pass a test but not to the degree necessary to apply it to other areas of one's life or to connect it meaningfully to real-life challenges. At their best, students are "curious, vital, and self-motivated. ... striving to learn; extend themselves; master new skills; and apply their talents responsibly" (Ryan & Deci, 2000, p. 68). The type of environment that brings out their best, according to Ryan and Deci (2000), is one that meets their needs for competence, autonomy, and relatedness. When students inhabit learning environments that provide meaningful tasks they are capable of attaining, their innate need for competence is met, and they are likely to experience a level of authentic motivation that leads them to invest greater levels of effort and, thus, be more successful. Eccles and Wigfield's (2002) expectancy-value theory of motivation adds that when such tasks enable students to reach valued goals, their motivation is enhanced even more.

Expecting that one is capable of reaching a valued goal is not the whole story of motivation, however. Along with competence needs, students also have psychological needs for relatedness and autonomy (Ryan & Deci, 2000). Even when a student may not value a learning task or goal, if others who are important to him or her value the goal, it can provide the motivational fuel that sustains effort (Eccles & Wigfield, 2002; Ryan & Deci, 2000). Offering students appropriate choices for demonstrating their learning can also enhance self-determined motivation because it supports their need for autonomy. Self-determined motivation has the added benefit of leading to increased persistence when the task is difficult, as well as better performance and well-being (Ryan & Deci, 2000).

Despite the important role motivation plays in learning, many college classroom environments are not designed to bring out the best in students. Strengths-oriented teaching builds on these theories and principles of motivation to do just that. When students become aware of the assets they already possess that can help them reach their learning goals, a positive energy is created that enhances creativity and complex problem solving (Fredrickson, 2001) and fosters a sense of competence. Identifying and affirming students' strengths highlight specific additional pathways toward reaching valued goals, increasing students' expectation that they are capable of attaining them (Lopez, 2004). Possessing these heightened expectations, motivation is improved, and students are likely to invest greater effort in the learning process.

Strengths Development

Grounded in positive psychology (Seligman & Csikszentmihalyi, 2000), with connections in social work (Saleebey, 2006), business (Clifton & Harter, 2003; Luthans, Youssef, & Avolio, 2007), and the talent development philosophy in higher education advocated by Kuh, Kinzie, Schuh, Whitt, and Associates (2005), a strengths development perspective seeks to capitalize on individuals' assets in order to help them lead productive, fulfilling lives. Within the context of higher education, such a perspective focuses on identifying and developing the potential that lies within each student (Lopez & Louis, 2009).

The field of positive psychology highlights optimal functioning of both individuals and communities, targeting for attention "the fulfilled individual and the thriving community" (Seligman & Csikszentmihalyi, 2000, p. 5). This emphasis on what is right with people and what is working well has led to a psychology of human strengths (Aspinwall & Staudinger, 2003) that investigates positive aspects of human well-being. In this context, strengths are defined as "the ability to flexibly apply as many different resources and skills as necessary to solve a problem or work toward a goal" (p. 13). This approach resonates with the perspective from the field of social work represented in Saleebey's (2006) focus on assets clients already possess that can be applied in a therapeutic setting to help them grow and succeed. Linley, Willars, and Biswas-Diener (2010) conceptualized strengths as things one does well and that energize him or her: It is both excellent performance and energy that define a strength.

Psychologists such as Peterson and Seligman (2004) have tended to focus more on *character strengths* in contrast to the *competence strengths* emphasized in business settings by Buckingham (2007) and Clifton and Harter (2003). In the context of strengths-oriented teaching, both perspectives offer helpful insights and strategies for instructors to leverage the potential of their students.

Character strengths, as conceptualized by Peterson and Seligman (2004), are the "psychological ingredients" or "distinguishable routes" (p. 13) to living a good life. These strengths are the building blocks of healthy individuals and communities, as they lead to the core virtues of wisdom, courage, humanity, justice, temperance, and transcendence valued by moral philosophers and religious thinkers universally and historically. Measured by the Values in Action Inventory of Strengths (VIA-IS; Seligman, Park, & Peterson, 2004), character strengths are trait-like; however, they are also influenced by environments and, thus, can be changed. Peterson and Seligman noted that *signature strengths* are the handful of traits that a person "owns, celebrates, and frequently exercises" (p. 18). By leveraging these natural tendencies in the classroom, instructors can capitalize on intrinsic motivation and natural interest that can lead to engaged learning.

An alternative view of strengths was originally proposed by Clifton and Nelson (1992) and measured by the Clifton StrengthsFinder (Gallup Organization, 1999). Clifton and Nelson defined strengths as patterns of "behavior, thoughts, and feelings that produce a high degree of satisfaction" (p. 42) and also lead to excellent performance in a particular activity. These strengths of competence enable a person to consistently perform at his or her best levels and accomplish valued tasks. The assumption is that everyone has naturally recurring patterns that can be productively applied. Conceptualized as *natural talents,* these patterns often include ways of processing information, perceiving the world, or interacting with people. Such talents can be developed into strengths when they are honed by knowledge and skills to produce consistent, near-perfect performance (Clifton, Anderson, & Schreiner, 2006). The emphasis in this perspective is on excellence, which many instructors may find to be a helpful approach to students' academic success.

Regardless of which definition of strengths is preferred or used, a *strengths philosophy* undergirds strengths-oriented teaching. A strengths philosophy is characterized by a set of beliefs about human potential and motivation, as well as by a commitment to bringing out the best in others. Strengths-oriented educators believe that all students have the potential to learn and grow and that it is possible to create learning opportunities to foster that potential (Lopez & Louis, 2009). This philosophy is congruent with the *talent development approach* advocated by Kuh et al. (2005) as one of the best strategies for facilitating student success. A talent development approach "refers to the notion that every student can learn under the right conditions" (p. 77) and is characterized by arranging the learning environment to "maximize student potential so that students leave college different in desired ways from how they started" (p. 77).

However, it is not sufficient to identify students' strengths; the key to success lies in developing those strengths and applying them to the academic challenges students face. Strengths development entails not only identifying the natural talents and assets students bring with them to the learning environment but also teaching students how to invest effort and practice to hone those talents into consistently excellent performance (Louis, 2011). Learning to apply their strengths to new or challenging situations enables students to experience greater levels of success than would be possible otherwise. In research with first-year students, Louis (2011) found that a strengths-development approach led to greater psychological and academic benefits than merely identifying and affirming students' strengths, emphasizing the importance of helping students refine and apply their strengths to academic tasks.

Within this philosophical foundation, strengths-oriented teaching is defined as *leveraging the instructor's strengths and deliberately connecting students' strengths to strategies for mastering the course content, so that students are more motivated and engaged in the learning process.* This approach is characterized by six pedagogical practices that encourage engaged learning and are likely to increase students' academic success.

Strengths-Oriented Teaching Practices

These practices are specific strategies that instructors can adopt to enhance levels of engaged learning among students in their classrooms. Collectively, the six practices outlined below represent a more coherent and potentially different approach to university-level pedagogy than is often practiced.

Be aware of one's own strengths as an instructor and apply those strengths to each aspect of the teaching process. Strengths-oriented teaching begins with the instructor's awareness and appropriate application of his or her own strengths to the teaching process. When instructors are aware of the assets or talents they bring into the classroom and how those talents can be specifically and productively applied to enhance their ability to facilitate students' learning, they are better able to engage students in learning, enjoy teaching more (Liesveld, Miller, & Robison, 2005), and experience less stress (Wood, Linley, Maltby, Kashdan, & Hurling, 2011). As Fredrickson (2009) notes, "people who have the opportunity every day to do what they do best—to act on their strengths—are far more likely to flourish" (p. 189).

Instructors can become aware of their talents in various ways. Reflective journaling or discussing with others what energizes them, what they are passionate about, what is deeply satisfying, what comes easily, what they are doing when they lose track of time, or what they yearn to do can provide important clues to the presence of talent. Instruments, such as the Clifton StrengthsFinder (The Gallup Organization, 1999), the VIA-IS (Selgiman, Park, & Peterson, 2004), Realise2 (CAPP, 2010), and StandOut (Buckingham, 2012), can provide a valid, reliable, and faster method of identifying these natural talents that can be developed into teaching strengths. Each of these instruments provides respondents with a description of three to five dominant areas of talents that can be leveraged.

Once the dominant talent themes are identified, learning to apply those talents appropriately and productively to each aspect of the teaching process is the key to successful teaching. There are four specific components of teaching to which talents can be productively applied: (a) the course design and lesson planning process, (b) course delivery, (c) feedback and assessment, and (d) interpersonal rapport with students. Rather than adopting specific strategies that other instructors use, the best results are likely to occur when instructors customize their approach to teaching by creatively applying their own talents. To accomplish this task, instructors might ask themselves the following questions:

- How energized am I about each of these components of teaching? What is specifically satisfying to me about each one?
- When I am at my best as an instructor, what am I doing? When I am most fulfilled by teaching, what is happening at that moment?
- If I am not energized by a specific aspect of teaching, how could I apply one or more of my dominant talents to that challenge?
- When I have been successful in other arenas besides teaching, what led to that success? How could I apply that to a teaching challenge I am experiencing or to an area of teaching that does not energize me?

Careful exploration of how instructors can capitalize on their existing talents, honing them with additional knowledge and skills, can build their confidence and self-efficacy in the classroom and provide a foundation for enhancing students' learning. When such exploration occurs within a community of other instructors, the benefits are multiplied (Palmer, 1997; Schreiner & Louis, 2011).

Begin each course by explaining the strengths development philosophy and connecting it to one's teaching practices. The messages from an instructor on the first day of class set the tone for the course and can influence students' perceptions of their ability to succeed, which then affects their motivation to engage in learning (Perry, Hall, & Ruthig, 2005). On that first day, when the sense of control is at its lowest in students as they wonder what it will take for them to succeed in this particular class (Perry, 2003), it is important to communicate three specific messages: (a) there are strategies that can help students master the course content—and the instructor will share those strategies; (b) the instructor believes all students in the class are capable of learning the material if they invest quality effort and use the right strategies; and (c) all students bring with them to the course specific talents that, when combined with strategic practice, will help them succeed.

These messages are supported by Bain's (2004) research, which found that the best university instructors believe students want to learn and can do so successfully. As part of their pedagogical practice, they regularly "shared with students their secrets about learning" (p. 141). Such beliefs and communication of strategies serve a two-fold purpose: (a) they convey to students that instructors believe they can succeed, which is a powerful motivating force, and (b) they send the message that it is possible to succeed in the course, which supports students' needs for competence. When instructors communicate that the investment of effort and strategic practice will lead to success, they are teaching students that their abilities are changeable with hard work—what Dweck (2006) called a *growth mindset*. Her research has demonstrated that teaching students to have a growth mindset leads to higher levels of motivation, greater levels of effort, a focus on learning for its own sake, and ultimately deeper learning.

A specific example of this strategy is an activity for the first day of class. Instructors can begin by displaying photos of highly successful athletes, musicians, and other accomplished experts who would be readily recognized by students and then ask what these "best of the best" have in common. As students brainstorm and the instructor writes their input on the board, a pattern should emerge: These people, who are at the top of their fields, all have talent—and they all practice a lot! The instructor can then relate specific stories about each exemplar, noting how they invested effort to develop their natural talents into consistently near-perfect performance. A short lesson might also be included that teaches students how the brain physically changes as a result of practice (see Bransford, Brown, & Cocking, 2008). For example, cognitive neuroscientists have demonstrated that the brain rewires itself with concentrated attention and repetitive practice; the old adage "practice makes perfect" seems to describe the way the brain can change. When students learn about this brain plasticity, it can encourage them to invest effort in the strategies needed for success. Additionally, instructors could share, to the degree they feel comfortable doing so, their own talent themes as part of introducing themselves to the class and articulate how each strength has helped them approach their discipline or the teaching process. For example, one introductory chemistry instructor brings in a panel of chemists and chemistry professors, who describe their own unique strengths and how they use them to be successful in their profession. The instructor concludes by emphasizing to students how different the panel members' strengths are and that there is not a particular strengths profile necessary for success—it is how the professionals applied their talents to their work that made all the difference.

Finally, research has provided evidence that when people are given meaningful explanations for required tasks, they are more likely to approach such tasks with higher levels of motivation and effort (Ryan & Deci, 2000). Particularly within the college classroom, explaining to students why an instructor has selected particular assignments or classroom practices—and what the instructor hopes students will learn in the process—can enhance engaged learning. When those explanations occur within a context where the strengths philosophy is foundational to the selection of every practice, it conveys to students the instructor's desire to bring out their best and help them learn, which encourages them to invest the necessary effort in the learning process.

Provide opportunities for students to identify their strengths; then, connect students to other students, encouraging them to explore how their strengths interact with the strengths of others. In addition to instructors recognizing and applying their own strengths to the practice of teaching, a strengths-oriented approach encourages students to explore their strengths, as well. However, this practice does not mean that class time is taken to identify students' talents or that instructors must know the strengths of every student in the classroom. Strengths identification is primarily the student's job; the instructor simply provides the means and opportunity outside of class to begin that process and then structures classroom experiences and assignments so that students learn how their strengths contribute to their success and affect others.

The strengths-identification process has been outlined earlier in this chapter. Within the context of a classroom setting, instructors could require students to complete an online instrument outside of class (resources and websites are listed at the end of this chapter), journal about their previous successes and what contributed to them, or answer a set of questions about what is energizing or fulfilling to them. By requiring this work outside of class, the instructor conveys that strengths identification is an important part of succeeding in the course. Particularly when the instructor has already laid the groundwork by explaining the strengths philosophy the first day of class, these assignments will connect naturally in students' minds to mastering the course content.

Because relatedness is a fundamental human need that must be met for self-authored motivation to occur (Ryan & Deci, 2000), strengths-oriented teaching practices capitalize on relationships in and out of the classroom. In the classroom, the instructor fosters relationships with each student and also among the students as a whole, creating a sense of community that bolsters student motivation and commitment to learning. As students engage in group projects, one of the first tasks can be for each group member to articulate his or her talents and how they will contribute to the final product. Michaelsen and Sweet (2008), in their extensive description of the best practices in team-based learning, suggested that students be strategically organized into permanent groups for the term. They recommended these teams be as diverse as possible, yet given substantive opportunity to form relationships with one another over the course of the term. When groups are assigned on the basis of diverse strengths and what can be contributed to the group's products and processes, and when groups are given instructions regarding how to capitalize on members' strengths to accomplish their goals, team-based learning can become even more effective.

Incorporate teaching practices that resonate with the learning styles and strengths of students in the classroom. Kuh et al. (2005) noted the most engaging academic environments are characterized by faculty who know their students and how they learn, including "their preferred learning styles, their talents, and when and where they need help" (p. 301). Although it may be virtually impossible for an instructor to remember each individual student's learning style and talent constellation, there are two basic principles that undergird this teaching strategy: (a) instructors remember there are different learning styles and talents in the room and (b) instructors design classroom activities and structure the course in such a way there is an activity or assignment that resonates with each style. For example, if learning styles are conceived as modalities used to perceive and input information for learning (Fleming & Mills, 1992), then each class session could include an aspect that speaks to the visual learners (e.g., concept mapping, drawing diagrams on the board), the auditory learners (e.g., class discussion, minilectures on key concepts), the reading-and-writing learners (e.g., PowerPoint presentations, handouts), and the kinesthetic learners (e.g., videos, demonstrations).

To incorporate teaching practices that resonate with students' strengths, it may be helpful for instructors to create a matrix of the strengths in the classroom. This process is particularly useful when students have been required to complete a strengths inventory outside of class. They can e-mail the instructor their results, which are then placed into the class matrix. In this way, the instructor not only has a list of each student's strengths for future reference but also has a sense of how the strengths themes are distributed across the class. For example, if an instructor notes there is an abundance of socially oriented talent themes, classroom activities may be more directed toward class discussion and group work. If, on the other hand, the instructor notes a preponderance of strengths themes that are more analytical, intellective, and reflective, classroom activities can be arranged for personal reflection or dyadic conversations rather than large group discussions. Again, knowing the specific strengths constellation of each individual student is less important than remembering to offer a variety of classroom experiences for the different strengths represented in the class.

Design meaningful assignments that allow students to connect their strengths to the learning goals of the course. Self-determination and authentic motivation flourish in environments that not only meet students' needs for competence and relatedness but also their need for autonomy (Ryan & Deci, 2000). In this context, autonomy is not independence but rather the opportunity to exercise one's ability to make thoughtful choices about the best way to master the course content. When students are given a variety of methods for meeting the learning goals of a course and demonstrating mastery, motivation is bolstered. When those options can be intentionally linked to students' strengths, the motivational benefit is enhanced even further because another layer of meaningfulness is added. To whatever extent students can perceive their assignments as chosen and relevant to valued goals, they are more likely to experience engaged learning (Schreiner, Hulme, Hetzel, & Lopez, 2009).

The degree of choice, as well as the opportunities for choice, can vary by the level of the course. For example, instructors of large introductory courses may need to limit the opportunities for choice to selecting between two questions on an essay exam or allowing students to write their own bonus question that can substitute for one item they missed on the exam. In smaller introductory-level courses, students might also be permitted to choose among two or three specific options for their major assignment; in upper-level courses, those choices could be expanded such that the student writes a proposal to the instructor articulating how he or she will demonstrate course mastery in the major assignment. Part of the proposal would include explicitly linking the student's strengths to the assignment in order to justify the particular choice. Providing choices within a mastery context does not negate the need for instructors to continue to provide clear expectations and parameters for the assignment, however. When students receive clear expectations and examples, along with a rubric describing how the work will be evaluated, they are well equipped to create an assignment that will meet the learning goals of a course.

Provide timely, instructive feedback to students throughout the course, linking students' performance to their talents and effort where appropriate. Frequent feedback is essential for learning to occur (Zull, 2002). Such feedback provides students with the information they need to modify future performance. Therefore, the best feedback is frequent, timely, clear and specific, and instructive. Frequent feedback allows the student to make constant small corrections along the way rather than coming to the end of a course and discovering that major corrections are needed. Timely feedback is given to students before the next assignment is due so they can demonstrate a higher level of learning in that assignment. Clear and specific feedback that is instructive provides students with concrete, positive suggestions for improving the assignment, articulating what needs to be changed, and how to do so.

Strengths-oriented teaching takes feedback one step further (Louis & Schreiner, 2012). Although providing timely instructive feedback is a natural outgrowth of the desire to bring out the best in students, strengths-oriented educators also attempt to link their feedback in positive ways to students' talents and effort. For example, noting where students have grown and affirming the level of effort evidenced in the assignment reflects a strengths philosophy. Employing greater specificity and tying the observed improvements to the use of particular talents or strengths is an advanced application of the strengths philosophy, one that is more easily done in smaller classes where instructors have a matrix of the strengths of each student.

A final way in which feedback can be linked to students' strengths is in debriefing the assignment with the student in person. For example, some instructors schedule 15-minute meetings with each student once or twice each term, particularly after major assignments or exams are returned, and require those meetings as part of the course expectations outlined in the syllabus. During these debriefing meetings, students are asked how they went about completing the assignment or studying for the test. They are then asked to link their chosen strategies to their strengths: How did their approach align with their natural talents? Often instructors discover that students who are not performing well are using strategies that might not be a good fit for their own talents; this debriefing provides an opportunity to explore with the student a more effective strategy.

Conclusion

Strengths-oriented teaching represents a paradigm shift for many instructors. Rather than focusing on students' deficits and attempting to remediate them, strengths-oriented teaching recognizes the talents students bring to the learning environment and uses those talents as the foundation for further learning—and for addressing academic challenges. Strengths-oriented teachers, above all else, believe their students are capable of learning under the right conditions and attempt to create those conditions in their classrooms. They desire to bring out the best in their students, and they do so by applying their own natural talents to each aspect of the teaching process. In addition, they communicate to students there are strategies for success and that it is part of their job to teach students those strategies. Strengths-oriented instructors take the time to know their students and how they learn; they also foster students' self-awareness of strengths and provide opportunities for students to learn to apply their strengths to the course content. Further, a strengths-oriented classroom is structured around practices that help students demonstrate mastery, creating a community of learners who are committed to one another and engaged in learning together. In the process, students are provided with appropriate choices; meaningful connections to the course content, fellow students, and the instructor; and concrete strategies for success. These strengths-oriented practices, thus, become pathways to engaged learning that last far beyond the final exam and can impact students for a lifetime.

Resources

www.apu.edu/strengthsacademy—home of the Noel Strengths Academy, a clearinghouse at Azusa Pacific University for resources and research on strengths-oriented approaches within higher education

www.strengthsquest.com—sponsored by the Gallup Organization and location of the Clifton StrengthsFinder, along with substantive educational resources on the use of the results

www.viacharacter.org—homepage of the VIA Character Survey, sponsored by the VIA Institute on Character

www.strengths2020.com—location of the Realise2 instrument, sponsored by the Centre for Applied Positive Psychology in the UK

www.tmbc.com—the Marcus Buckingham Company homepage and location of the StandOut instrument, along with resources oriented toward strengths-based leadership

References

Anderson, E. C., Cantwell, L., & Schreiner, L. A. (2004). *Strengths-based teaching.* Retrieved from www.apu.edu/strengthsacademy

Aspinwall, L. G., & Staudinger, U. M. (Eds.). (2003). *A psychology of human strengths: Fundamental questions and future directions for a positive psychology.* Washington, DC: American Psychological Association.

Bain, K. (2004). *What the best college teachers do.* Cambridge, MA: Harvard University Press.

Biggs, J. B. (2003). *Teaching for quality learning at university.* Buckingham, UK: Open University Press.

Bransford, J. D., Brown, A. L., & Cocking, R. R. (2008). Mind and brain. In K. Fischer and M. H. Immordino-Yang (Eds.), *The Jossey-Bass reader on the brain and learning* (pp. 89-105). San Francisco, CA: Jossey-Bass.

Buckingham, M. (2007). *Go put your strengths to work.* New York, NY: The Free Press.

Buckingham, M. (2012). *StandOut.* Retrieved from http://standout.tmbc.com/assets/misc/StandOutTechnical_Summary.pdf

Centre for Applied Positive Psychology (CAPP). (2010). *Realise2.* Retrieved from http://www.strengths2020.com

Clifton, D. O., Anderson, E. C., & Schreiner, L. A. (2006). *StrengthsQuest: Discover and develop your strengths in academics, career, and beyond (2nd ed.).* Washington, DC: The Gallup Organization.

Clifton, D. O., & Harter, J. K. (2003). Investing in strengths. In K. S. Cameron, J. E. Dutton, & R. E. Quinn (Eds.), *Positive organizational scholarship* (pp. 111-121). San Francisco, CA: Berrett-Koehler.

Clifton, D. O., & Nelson, P. (1992). *Soar with your strengths.* New York, NY: Dell.

Dweck, C. (2006). *Mindset: The new psychology of success.* New York, NY: Random House.

Eccles, J. S., & Wigfield, A. (2002). Motivational beliefs, values, and goals. *Annual Review of Psychology, 53,* 109-132.

Fleming, N. D., & Mills, C. (1992). Helping students understand how they learn. *The Teaching Professor, 7*(4). Madison, WI: Magma.

Fredrickson, B. L. (2001).The role of positive emotions in positive psychology: The broaden-and-build theory of positive emotions. *American Psychologist, 56*(3), 218-226.

Fredrickson, B. L. (2009). *Positivity.* New York, NY: Crown.

Gallup Organization. (1999). *Clifton StrengthsFinder.* Washington, DC: Author.

Kuh G. D., Kinzie, J., Schuh, J. H., Whitt, E. J., & Associates. (2005). *Student success in college: Creating conditions that matter.* San Francisco, CA: Jossey-Bass.

Liesveld, R., Miller, J., & Robison, J. (2005). *Teach with your strengths: How great teachers inspire their students.* New York, NY: Gallup.

Linley, A., Willars, J., & Biswas-Diener, R. (2010). *The strengths book.* Coventry, UK: CAPP Press.

Lopez, S. (2004, January). *Naming, nurturing, and navigating: Capitalizing on strengths in daily life.* Paper presented at the Gallup Organization conference on Building a Strengths-Based Campus, Omaha, NE.

Lopez, S. J., & Louis, M. C. (2009). The principles of strengths-based education. *Journal of College and Character, 10*(4), 1-8.

Louis, M. C. (2011). Strengths interventions in higher education: The effect of identification versus development approaches on implicit self-theory. *The Journal of Positive Psychology, 6*(3), 204-215.

Louis, M. C., & Schreiner, L. A. (2012). Helping students thrive: A strengths development model. In L. A. Schreiner, M. C. Louis, & D. D. Nelson (Eds.), *Thriving in transitions: A research-based approach to college student success* (pp. 19-40). Columbia, SC: University of South Carolina, National Resource Center for The First-Year Experience & Students in Transition.

Luthans, F., Youssef, C. M., & Avolio, B. J. (2007). *Psychological capital: Developing the human competitive edge.* New York, NY: Oxford University Press.

Michaelsen, L. K., & Sweet, M. (2008). The essential elements of team-based learning. *New Directions for Teaching and Learning, 116,* 7-27.

Palmer, P. J. (1997). *The courage to teach: Exploring the inner landscape of a teacher's life*. San Francisco, CA: Jossey-Bass.

Perry, R. P. (2003). Perceived (academic) control and causal thinking in achievement settings: Markers and mediators. *Canadian Psychologist, 44*(4), 312-331.

Perry, R. P., Hall, N. C., & Ruthig, J. C. (2005). Perceived (academic) control and scholastic attainment in higher education. In J. C. Smart (Ed.), *Higher education: Handbook of theory and research* (Vol. 20, pp. 363-436). The Netherlands: Springer.

Peterson, C., & Seligman, M. (2004). *Character strengths and virtues: A handbook and classification*. New York, NY: Oxford University Press; Washington, DC: American Psychological Association.

Pintrich, P. R., & Zusho, A. (2002). Student motivation and self-regulated learning in the college classroom. In J. C. Smart & W. G. Tierney (Eds.), *Higher education: Handbook of theory and research* (Vol. 16, pp. 55-128). The Netherlands: Springer.

Ryan, R. M., & Deci, E. L. (2000). Self-determination theory and the facilitation of intrinsic motivation, social development, and well-being. *American Psychologist, 55*(1), 68-78.

Saleebey, D. (2006). Introduction: Power in the people. In D. Saleebey (Ed.), *The strengths perspective in social work practice* (4th ed., pp. 1-24). Boston, MA: Pearson.

Schreiner, L., Hulme, E., Hetzel, R., & Lopez, S. (2009). Positive psychology on campus. In S. J. Lopez & C. R. Snyder (Eds.), *Oxford handbook of positive psychology*, (2nd ed., pp. 569–578). New York, NY: Oxford University Press.

Schreiner, L., & Louis, M. C. (2011). The Engaged Learning Index: Implications for faculty development. *Journal of Excellence in College Teaching, 22*(1), 5-28.

Seligman, M. E. P., & Csikszentmihalyi, M. (2000). Positive psychology: An introduction. *American Psychologist, 55*, 51-82.

Seligman, M. E. P., Park, N., & Peterson, C. (2004). The Values in Action (VIA) classification of character strengths. *Ricerche di Psicologia, 27*(1), 63-78.

Tagg, J. (2003). *The learning paradigm college*. Bolton, MA: Anker.

Wood, A. M., Linley, P. A., Maltby, J., Kashdan, T. B., & Hurling, R. (2011). Using personal and psychological strengths leads to increases in well-being over time: A longitudinal study and the development of the strengths use questionnaire. *Personality and Individual Differences, 50*(1), 15-19.

Zull, J. E. (2002). *The art of changing the brain: Enriching the practice of teaching by exploring the biology of learning*. Sterling, VA: Stylus.

Chapter 7
Interactive Group Learning

James E. Groccia, Emad A. Ismail, and S. Raj Chaudhury

Often when students hear they will be doing group work, they cringe. They interpret this teaching approach as a way of transferring the burden of work from faculty to students or, even worse, relate it to previously unsuccessful group experiences (e.g., poor group dynamics, unequal distribution of work). However, when structured correctly and designed carefully, group learning strategies can provide comfortable, low-threat learning environments that benefit all students. Research shows that students working in small groups learn more and retain information longer, enhance their social interaction skills, and are more satisfied with their classes (Chickering & Gamson, 1991; Johnson, Johnson, & Smith, 1991; Springer, Stanne, & Donovan, 1999). In addition to significant and substantial gains in learning, working interactively helps students obtain deeper levels of understanding (Mergendoller, Bellisimo, & Maxwell, 2000; Pattanpichet, 2011; Terenzini, Cabrera, Colbeck, Parente, & Bjorklund, 2001). Thus, group-learning activities (both collaborative and cooperative) engender significant real-world outcomes and provide a more inclusive and dynamic education, especially when diverse learners are involved (Ashton-Hay & Pillay, 2010).

There is much confusion in the literature regarding the terms *collaborative learning* and *cooperative learning*, with some authors using the words interchangeably and others identifying them as distinct methods. Collaborative and cooperative learning are both forms of group learning that emphasize small-group student involvement over passive, lecture-based teaching, and each focuses on completion of a specific learning task (Panitz, 1999; Pattanpichet, 2011). For the purposes of this chapter, the more inclusive term *interactive group learning* is used to describe both collaborative and cooperative techniques that emphasize the social nature of learning and facilitate joint intellectual effort by two or more students, or students and teachers together. Borrowing from both collaborative and cooperative learning definitions, interactive group learning is further characterized as a "coordinated, synchronous activity that is the result of a continued attempt to construct and maintain a shared conception of a problem" (Roschelle & Teasley, 1995, p. 70). This chapter begins with a discussion of the historical and theoretical underpinnings, characteristics, and elements of these methods followed by examples of effective interactive group learning strategies.

Historical and Theoretical Underpinnings

Interactive group learning approaches were relatively underused in higher education up until the late 1970s, partially due to a prevailing academic culture that promoted a "survival of the fittest" approach of interpersonal competition (Johnson & Johnson, 2009, p. 365). College instruction was delivered primarily through lecture, and grading was based on a normal distribution paradigm, which pitted students against each other for a place on the bell-shaped curve. Criticism of this style was first noted in the 1960s (Sexton, 1961), and some faculty, influenced by operant conditioning and behavior modification (Skinner, 1968) as well as the rise of student self-empowerment and activism, began using *personalized systems of instruction* (PSI; Keller, 1968) that enabled students to learn independently of other students. In PSI, students complete small, sequential units of material at their own pace; demonstrate mastery of the material in the unit before proceeding to the next unit; receive reinforcement for correct responses or opportunities to restudy; and retest until the accepted level of success or knowledge is attained (Pear, Schnerch, Silva, Svenningsen, & Lambert, 2011). This form of learning, as well as that fostered through the lecture (still the predominant form of university instruction), largely ignored the role of peer interaction and social relationships in learning.

Interactive group learning and teaching techniques historically emanate from the writings of John Dewey (1963), who suggested that education should be viewed as "a social enterprise in which all individuals have opportunities to contribute and to which all feel a responsibility" (p. 61). This approach was advanced by Vygotsky's (1978) theory of social constructivism that posits social interaction plays a fundamental role in the development of cognition and learning, and is further supported by recent research on the social brain (Mercer, 2013).

Psychology and anthropology researchers have proposed that the distinctive nature of human thinking and learning is the product of our evolution as social beings; humans are born with social brains that enable us to manage complex social relationships in ways other animals cannot (Mercer, 2013). The social brain has a "constant orientation to others" and creates meaning "through brains interacting, rather than through the operation of individual internal cognition" (Royal Society of Arts, 2010, p. 2). Social interactions help us learn the skills necessary to survive and are critical today for educational success—going beyond the mere transmission and acquisition of facts and skills and including the ability to interact with others to justify opinions, analyses, solutions, and conclusions (Mercer, 2013).

Characteristics of Interactive Group Learning

The umbrella term interactive group learning encompasses a learner-centered approach focusing on the students' exploration or application of the course material and not just finding the instructor's right answer. It "shifts the responsibility for learning away from the teacher as expert to the student" and allows students to have more control in forming friendship and interest groups (Panitz, 1999, para. 9). Students engage in their own knowledge construction by integrating new information gained through social interaction into the community's knowledge networks (Ku, Tseng, & Akarasriworn, 2013). Participation in an interactive learning group is, in a way, a re-educational process that supports learners in their efforts to become members of the classroom knowledge community whose common property is different from that of knowledge communities to which they already belong (Bruffee, 1995). This approach creates opportunities for learners to socially construct knowledge within an interactive community of learners (Oxford, 1997) where

- learning is an active endeavor;
- learning depends on engaging students in challenging tasks or questions;
- learners are diverse;
- learning is inherently social (i.e., it is through talking and interaction among students that learning occurs); and
- learning has affective and subjective dimensions, as it is socially involving and emotionally demanding (Smith & MacGregor, 1992).

In an interactive learning scenario, students may be assigned group roles (e.g., recorder, spokesperson, supporter, skeptic, researcher, summarizer) by the instructor, or they may divide tasks among themselves. In both cases, "cooperation is typically accomplished through the division of labor, with each person responsible for some portion of the problem solving" (Lai, 2011, p. 6). Further, students may be assessed individually or as a team.

According to Matthews and colleagues (1995), collaborative and cooperative learning (i.e., interactive group learning) share these common features:

- teacher acts as a facilitator;
- teaching and learning experiences are shared by teacher and student;
- focus is on higher-order cognitive skills (e.g., analysis, expressing reasoned opinions);
- emphasis is placed on students' responsibility for their own learning;
- students engage in articulating ideas in small groups;
- students develop social and teambuilding skills;
- students' cognitive, cultural, social, and experiential diversity are used; and
- students' academic success and information retention are increased.

Designing Effective Interactive Group Learning

Interactive learning activities can be most effective when they incorporate the following characteristics, which are described in more detail below: interpersonal and small-group skills, pre-activity preparation, promotive interaction, positive participant interdependence, peer assessment, group and individual accountability, and group processing (Felder & Brent, 2007; Johnson, Johnson, & Holubec, 1991; Tomcho & Foels, 2012). Including these elements into the design of interactive group-learning activities will enhance their effectiveness and maximize positive outcomes.

Interpersonal and small-group skills are critical for students to be able to function effectively in interactive learning groups. Interactive skills include leadership, decision making, trust building, communication, and conflict-management techniques. These skills need to be taught as purposefully and precisely as academic skills. One way to achieve this goal is for students within a group to be assigned or assume differentiated roles, such as recorder, coordinator, timekeeper, and presenter, which each require different proficiencies (Smith, 1996). In addition, having group members periodically switch roles offers students an opportunity to develop multiple skill sets.

Pre-activity preparation for interactive group learning involves using some form of practice or activity in which students' prior knowledge is activated. This can help students prepare before engaging in the interactive learning activity (Gagne & Driscoll, 1988). Preparation may include (a) having students complete a worksheet or a knowledge quiz prior to the learning activity, (b) beginning each class with a clicker quiz on assigned readings, or (c) providing a set of problems to be solved in the online course management system before class. Michaelsen and Sweet's (2011) use of the readiness assurance process in team-based learning (described later in this chapter) is another example of a pre-activity to engage students in group learning endeavors.

Promotive interaction takes place when students support each other's learning. Students explain, discuss, and teach what they know to classmates in groups where they can talk through each aspect of the assignment. This can create opportunities for students with varying levels of understanding, preparation, and prior knowledge to increase their learning as a result of interaction with others who have a greater understanding of the material being discussed (Hogan & Tudge, 1999; Slavin, 1996).

Positive participant interdependence is described by Johnson, Johnson, and Smith (1991) as the

> striving for mutual benefit so that all members of the group benefit from each other's efforts (your success benefits me and my success benefits you), their recognizing that all group members share a common fate (we sink or swim together) and that one's performance depends mutually on oneself and one's colleagues (we cannot do it without you), and their feeling proud and jointly celebrating when a group member is recognized for achievement (you got an A! that's terrific!). (p. 3)

Student interaction that promotes positive interdependence may also facilitate student learning outcomes, such as learning how to, when to, and the value of working both independently and on a team (Skilton, Forsyth, & White, 2008).

Peer assessment, both individual and group-focused, can lead to better learning by encouraging group members to take responsibility for their own learning efforts as well as those of the group (Gueldenzoph & May, 2002). Such assessment encourages students to attend to the material being learned and facilitates development of critical thinking (Cathey, 2007; Dunn, 2000). An example of a peer assessment technique (i.e., multiplier method) is presented in Figure 7. 1.

This method allows for each member of the learning group to assess all group members in terms of contribution to the overall task. (See Chapter 9 for additional information on assessment.)

Group and individual accountability is encouraged with the multiplier assessment method. When all group members are held responsible for goal attainment or outcome, the members are more likely to be engaged (Schlenker & Weigold, 1989), leading to better learning outcomes. Similarly, group outcomes are more likely to be of higher quality when all individuals participate in learning activities created to attain these outcomes. In addition to group assessment methods, instructors can further evaluate individual accountability in group projects by giving individual tests or assignments or randomly selecting one group member to give the answer.

Group processing is a way for group members to maintain effective working relationships as well as discuss how well they are achieving their goals. Project participants can be asked to (a) list at least three member actions that helped the group be successful and/or (b) list one action that could be added to make the group even more successful tomorrow. In addition, the instructor can provide valuable information as to how well groups are working together as individual units and within the class as a whole (Johnson, Johnson, & Smith, 1991).

Designing effective interactive group learning does not happen in vacuum. It is a multilayered process requiring planning and input from the instructor to identify and/or assign specific roles and assignments that can enhance interdependence, preparation of pre-activities to engage students' prior knowledge and class readiness, and careful supervision of groups to ensure promotive interaction.

Factors Influencing Interactive Group Learning

Predictably, not all applications of interactive group learning produce similar student learning outcomes. Three factors—group size, group duration, and task complexity—might explain variability in learning outcomes (Tomcho & Foels, 2012) and should be considered when designing interactive group learning approaches.

Group Size

Research indicates that group size affects student performance: As group size increases, performance decreases (Wheelan, 2009). However, the literature is not conclusive on the optimal group size for integrative learning, though most educators use groups that have three to six (Lim & Klein, 2006) or five to seven members (Michaelsen, 2002a). When groups get larger than this, the tendency for *social loafing*—where students expend less effort on a group project while expecting to benefit from the work—increases (Latane, Williams, & Harkins, 1979).

Written Group Reports:

Each group must hand in a written report for each problem. The report grade will be multiplied by the "multiplier" to determine your individual grade (e.g. 80/100 points for the report multiplied by a multiplier of 0.90 = 72 points for your personal grade). The multiplier (0.90 in this example) will be determined by the students in your group grading the relative efforts of themselves and their partners. Each student will distribute 100% of the group effort to each of the students in the group. Each person's evaluation of him/herself will not be used directly, while the remaining evaluations will be pooled to determine the overall multiplier for each individual. See the sample calculation below for a four-person group.

Sample Group Self-Evaluation Form

	Students evaluated			
Evaluator	**Adams**	**Boyd**	**Carlson**	**Dunn**
Adams	25	25	30	20
Boyd	25	25	25	25
Carlson	20	20	50	10
Dunn	25	25	30	20
Sum	*70*	*70*	*85*	*60*

Comments:

The strikeouts eliminate the grade each student gives to him/herself. For each student, the evaluations from all other group members are summed, and divided by the total possible points if each evaluator had assigned an equal point value (in this case, 25; in the case of a 5-person group, 20) to each group member (100% total). If the written report grade was 80, the multiplier and grades for each student would be

Adams:	70/75 = .93	GRADE = 0.93 X 80 = 74.4
Boyd:	70/75 = .93	GRADE = 0.93 X 80 = 74.4
Carlson:	85/75 = 1.13*	GRADE = 1.00 X 80 = 80.0
Dunn:	55/75 = .73	GRADE = 0.73 X 80 = 58.4

*Note: No one can receive a multiplier of greater than one (1.00), unless the group meets with the professor and presents a convincing case. Therefore, Carlson's multiplier of 1.13 defaults to 1.00.

Figure 7.1. Multiplier method for interactive group project grading.

Group Duration

Additionally, researchers have reported that group duration can have an impact on the group's performance (Levine & Moreland, 1999; Wheelan, Davidson, & Tilin, 2003; Yalom & Leszcz, 2005). Groups that meet for a limited amount of time may have students who are more likely to stay on task, achieve desired outcomes, and demonstrate less social loafing (Kelly & McGrath, 1985). Tomcho and Foels (2012) found groups that met for a brief time (i.e., 1-3 class sessions) demonstrated better learning than groups that met for longer periods, with the extended groups showing lower overall performance. However, if the nature and number of tasks are regularly changed and broken down into small units, strategically formed permanent groups lasting a semester can be key for successful team-based learning (Michaelsen & Sweet, 2011). Further, permanent groups can be effective learning environments if the groups are reconstituted regularly for brief activities (Tomacho & Foels, 2012).

Task Complexity

The type of task in which students are engaged also influences the outcomes of interactive group learning. Campbell (1988) identified five task types (i.e., decision, judgment, problem, fuzzy, and simple) that could affect the design and impact of group learning. A *decision* task involves making a choice from among a set of alternatives in order to select the best answer, solution, or course of action. In interactive learning, a decision task could be a debate that involves presenting and evaluating different alternative outcomes from which the best is chosen by the debaters or expert panel (Carroll, 2006). *Judgment* tasks ask students to consider and integrate diverse sources of information and make predictions about the likelihood of some future outcome or event, such as a case study analysis (Hall & Seery, 2006). *Problem* tasks require students to find the best way to achieve a desired outcome from a multiplicity of paths and include anagrams, jigsaw puzzles, and chess problems (Campbell, 1988). *Fuzzy* tasks "involve selecting from several possible outcomes when there are multiple ways in which the desired outcome could be determined" (Tomcho & Foels, 2012, p. 160). An example would be a project assignment where students must design one new product from many different alternatives, using one production method chosen from several alternative methods (Campbell, 1988). Finally, *simple* tasks "contain none of the attributes of complexity previously identified" (Campbell, 1988, p. 46), and are often straightforward, use a prescribed formula, and/or yield only one correct answer (e.g., What is the square root of 9?).

Effective Interactive Group Learning Approaches

Although there are many strategies that involve group work, this section offers examples of the most common interactive learning strategies. While some of the strategies described below have been used more commonly in certain fields, they all can be used effectively across disciplines.

Problem-Based Learning (PBL)

This instructional approach actively engages students in groups to solve complex, challenging problems to obtain required competencies or objectives and develop lifelong problem-solving skills (Engel, 1991). The problem is usually one that is ill-structured and complex, representing a real-world situation with multiple solutions rather than a single right answer that can easily be looked up. In addition, the problem often involves uncertainty as to which concepts or principles are necessary for the solution or which solution is best (Jonassen, 1997). Ommundsen (2001) further noted that unusual problems work best to capture student interest and attention.

Since PBL problems draw from real-world situations, the choices for content and topics are endless. Because of this, PBL has been used across the disciplines, including business education (Stinson & Milter, n. d.); economics (Farley, Erickson, Daly, 2005); engineering (Kolmos, Fink, & Krough, 2004); English, history, and environmental sciences (Stanford University, n.d.); medicine (Srinivasan, Wilkes, Stevenson, Nguyen, & Slavin, 2007); physics (Williams, 2001); and various science courses (Allen, Duch, & Groh, 1996; Ommundsen, 2001), to list a few.

The students' role in PBL is to (a) analyze available information, (b) apply prior knowledge and experience, (c) seek additional knowledge needed to effectively solve the problem, (d) consider all possible solutions, (d) make a decision, (f) analyze the factors related to this decision, (g) evaluate that solution, (h) defend their solutions with evidence, and (i) suggest ways to continue evaluating the new solution after implementation (Edens, 2000; Major & Palmer, 2001; Maudsley, 1999; Smith & MacGregor, 1992; Speck, 2003). Open-inquiry and self-discovery distinguish PBL from guided-inquiry, case-based learning (see below).

To begin the PBL process, students are prodded to look at the posed problem in light of existing knowledge and experience as well as analyze and discuss the problem from various perspectives by asking the question, What do we already know? This yields a problem statement that is used as a starting point for reaching a solution. The next question students must ask is, What do we need to know? That answer leads to a list of issues or questions that need to be answered or missing knowledge that is needed to resolve the problem. Through brainstorming, students dissect the problem into components and suggest working hypotheses and the best ways to collect needed information. They discuss and evaluate each hypothesis guided by the question, What should we do next? This results in a to-do list of resources to seek, articles to collect, videos to watch, experts to consult, and actions for each team member to take (SFSU, 2011). The solution to a PBL task can be as varied as the problem itself, resulting in a product; performance; piece of art or media; class, campus, or community presentation; service; diagnosis; or set of recommendations, to list a few. Similarly, assessment can incorporate a variety of methods (e.g., group or individual evaluation; formal or informal strategies; written, oral, or performance modes). Like the PBL task, for "assessments to be meaningful, they must have some connection to the real world" (SFSU, 2011, PBL Assessment Philosophy, para. 5).

PBL is not without its critics, however. One criticism is that due to student autonomy during the learning and assessment processes, the instructor's expertise and experience may not be efficiently or effectively incorporated (Roberts, Lawson, Newble, Self, & Chan, 2005). Further, in the absence of appropriate guidance, students may not be able to apply the material necessary for problem solving both in the class and in future practice. Despite these potential weaknesses, PBL offers an effective approach to improve student knowledge and outcomes through interactive group learning.

Case-Based Learning (CBL)

Case studies are narratives of real-life situations that set up a problem or unresolved tension. Similar to PBL, students are provided with a clinical problem and struggle to reach a solution. However, unlike PBL, both the students and instructor are responsible for reaching basic learning points; when students get stuck or off track, the instructor or the facilitator can offer guidance and suggestions. Students are also allowed to prepare in advance before class and ask questions during the session time. CBL, thus, provides more structure for the learner in an efficient, goal-directed manner (Srinivasan et al., 2007).

In addition to increasing engagement in class, the use of case studies helps improve problem-solving and critical-thinking skills, provides deeper understanding of concepts, and enhances the ability to make connections across multiple content areas (Herreid, 2011). While case studies can be incorporated into all disciplines, they are commonly used in the teaching of business, medicine, law, education, and engineering (Kim, Phillips, Pinsky, Brock, Phillips, & Keary, 2006). A good case is one that is relevant to the level of learner and objectives to be achieved, contains realistic and pertinent content, provides multiple perspectives, challenges with appropriate level of difficulty and complexity, considers student's prior knowledge, and includes suitable assessment and sound teaching aids (Kim et al., 2006). Case studies can reflect typical or atypical (i.e., outlier) situations and can be drawn from countless sources, including medical cases; business profiles; current events; and web depositories, such as The National Center for Case Study Teaching in Science's (NCCSTS, n.d.) peer-reviewed collection of over 400 cases in all areas of science and engineering.

Herreid (2011) stated that case study approaches vary depending on the way the narrative is presented. For example, he described the lecture method as a technique where the instructor is the storyteller (or performer), the information is presented in context, and the students remain passive recipients of knowledge. With a discussion approach, he noted the case can be presented through instructor-directed classroom discussion as well as more student-centered debates, symposia, mock trials, or public hearings. Herreid (2011) pointed out the similarities of the small-group case method with PBL and claimed this approach was useful for "promoting diversity of opinion and respect for divergent views and for improving the expression of ideas" (p. 32). Small-group cases can also incorporate the debate method (i.e., group members or teams argue a perspective with supporting evidence), which is effective in dealing with controversial topics; considering multiple viewpoints; and arriving at a judgment on topics such as stem cell research, creation versus evolution, or global warming (Herreid & DuRei, 2007). Other case study approaches Herreid (2011) identified include using individual cases (students work independently on a problem), computer simulations (computer-based interactive cases), and clicker cases (class discussion is conducted via clickers—especially useful in large classrooms).

Case studies can also be used for quick assessment of student learning. For example, an instructor can display a very brief case with a realistic situation on a PowerPoint slide or handout. Following the case description, students are asked questions, such as: What is the problem? What causes the problem? and How do you solve or prevent it? Students can work in pairs or in groups to discuss and record their answers. The instructor can then collect answers and, if time permits, call on some students to share their answers with class (Angelo & Cross, 1993).

Case studies are an effective way to help students understand a complex issue, and they can be used to extend the scope of knowledge or range of possible solutions for a topic. Herreid (2011) summed them up succinctly when he stated, "Case studies are stories with an educational message" (p. 31).

Team-Based Learning (TBL)

Originated by Larry Michaelsen in the late 1970s, TBL is an instructional strategy based on procedures for developing high-performance learning teams where individual work is done out of class and teamwork is completed in class. Students interact as in-class teams to apply content to simple and complex problems with the instructor providing feedback as the content expert. As with other learning approaches based on a case or problem, TBL has been implemented in a wide range of subjects and class formats, including accounting (Wilson, 1982); chemistry (Dinan & Frydrychowski, 1995); engineering (O'Connell, 2011); history (Restad, Onion, Reynolds, & Sweet, 2010); life sciences (McInerney, 2003); marketing (Hernandez, 2002); and medical and nursing education (Clark, Nguyen, Bray, & Levine, 2008; Haidet, O'Malley, & Richards, 2002), as well as in large classes across disciplines (Michaelsen, (2002b).

According to Michaelsen and Sweet (2008), "Team-based learning (TBL) possibly relies on small group interaction more heavily than any other commonly used instructional strategy in postsecondary education" (p. 7). They identified the four practical elements of TBL as:

1. Strategically formed, permanent teams
2. Readiness assurance
3. Application activities that promote both critical thinking and team development
4. Peer evaluation. (Michaelsen & Sweet, 2011, p. 41)

In the TBL approach, students begin a unit taking a short, multiple-choice test assessing their knowledge of pre-assigned readings and assignments (individual readiness assurance test—iRAT). In teams, they take the same exam again and must come to consensus on their team answers (team readiness assurance test—tRAT). They are provided with prompt feedback on their team responses using the immediate feedback assessment technique (IF-AT) scratch-off form (Epstein Educational Enterprises, n.d.), and teams can try multiple times to select the correct answer. In addition to correct and incorrect answers, IF-AT reveals the quality of the team's thought process in discussing the issue and which students had a better grasp of the topic.

The teams are then given an opportunity to appeal their incorrect answers by citing evidence from course materials. After this readiness-assurance process (RAP), the instructor reviews team tRAT scores to determine what concepts require further clarification and briefly lectures on misunderstood or incorrect content. The IF-AT forms also provide the instructor with a simple and fair grading mechanism (Karge, Phillips, Jessee, & McCabe, 2011). Students then complete carefully designed activities where they apply what they have learned during RAP to more complex problems or case studies. Michaelsen and Sweet (2011) suggested that all teams work on the same problem, case, or question and simultaneously report their solution choice. The process ends with peer evaluations of team members.

In TBL, content delivery shifts from the instructor to students helping each other. Michaelsen and Sweet (2011) claimed that "TBL enables instructors to achieve equal or better content coverage and still use 70 to 80 percent of class time with students engaged in activities that deepen understanding of how course content applies to real-life situations and problems" (p. 42). In addition, the RAP process, especially the tRAT, encourages students to interact using reciprocal teaching skills. "In their search for correct answers, students invariably alternate in and out of a teacher's role by asking each other the kinds of questions that the teacher normally would ask" (Michael & Sweet, 2011, p. 44).

Jigsaw

Jigsaw is an interactive group learning technique that promotes student participation and enthusiasm (Mengduo & Xiaoling, 2010) and encourages learning beyond individual reading or traditional lecture. It is especially useful in heavy content disciplines, such as engineering (Smith, 1995), history (Aronson, 2013), and natural sciences (Doymus, 2008; Popescu & Maftei, 2012). Using a jigsaw approach, each student is responsible for helping complete a puzzle by integrating his or her individual piece to create the whole. Further, every individual's involvement is required for full understanding and completion of the final product. The jigsaw technique encourages engagement, interdependence, and taking responsibility for both individual and group success in the learning process. The instructor's role, in addition to providing guidance during the activity, is to carefully choose the topic and divide it into subtopics to be used in the jigsaw groups.

For example, a jigsaw approach in teaching a history unit on World War II would begin with the instructor dividing the topic into subtopics (e.g., Hitler's prewar rise to power, the Holocaust, Britain's role in the war, the contribution of the Soviet Union, Japan's entry into the war, the development of the atomic bomb). After the class is divided into jigsaw groups, each group member is assigned a separate subtopic to research. Students from each group assigned the same subtopic convene to form expert groups to review and ensure they know the content well enough to return to their original group to teach other group members (Aronson, 2013).

Within the home group, each member serves as teacher for his or her subject area, making certain that other group members adequately grasp the content. Learners carefully listen and ask questions until they are confident of their learning. The final step in this teaching process is a test review and feedback session where the instructor debriefs students after the jigsaw activity is complete on both what has been learned and the jigsaw process itself (Johnson, Johnson, & Smith, 1991). As with other interactive group learning approaches, assessment can include both group and individual methods.

Think-Pair-Share

Think-pair-share, originated by Frank Lyman (1981) is a simple technique that allows students time to formulate answers or ideas and test those with other students before presenting them to the whole class. The strategy is also known as turn-to-your-partner (Johnson, Johnson, & Holubec, 1991) or turn-to-your-neighbor (Lundgren, 1994). Think-pair-share helps improve individual participation in class discussion, especially for shy students or nonnative speakers who typically remain silent in the classroom.

In this technique, the instructor states an open-ended question or presents a problem, and students must consider it alone for a brief time (1-2 minutes) and then turn to a neighbor to discuss their responses before settling on a final answer. After two to three minutes, the instructor reconvenes the class and calls on students to summarize and share the pair's responses to the whole class (Lyman, 1981).

Over the years, several researchers have introduced modifications to the think-share-pair method, such as

- **Think-Pair-Square-Share**—A pair of students turns to another pair (forming a square) and discusses what they have shared within their first pair before turning to the whole class (Millis & Cottell, 1998).
- **Think-Write-Pair-Share**—Students respond to a question by writing about it rather than reflecting, or they read a passage independently and then compose a written commentary. This method ensures that students are using academic vocabulary in both written and verbal form (Fisher, Brozo, Frey, & Ivey, 2007; Karge et al., 2011).
- **Alone-Together-Alone (ATA)**—Students begin by independently thinking about and writing down an answer to a question and then discuss their answer, in sequential order, with one other student, a larger group, and,

finally, the entire class. To complete the learning process, students return to their original written response and individually modify it based on the information shared by their classmates (Groccia, n.d.).

Use of the basic think-pair-share technique can be illustrated in a unit about global warming. The instructor shows the class an image of a melting iceberg and asks the students to describe and interpret the image. Students then briefly reflect on (or write about) the following questions: Have there been periods warmer than the present in the past? If so, when did such periods occur, and what is the evidence? Following individual reflection, students pair with each other to discuss their answers and then share with the class. The instructor can collect the responses and make it a basis for a class discussion or a short lecture on climate history.

Conclusion

Interactive group learning is an umbrella term for a variety of educational approaches, including collaborative and cooperative learning, involving joint intellectual effort by students in groups of two or more, or students and teachers together. It can be an effective approach for enhancing social skills and producing deeper and significant learning outcomes for diverse learners. Research has provided convincing evidence for the educational value of interactive group learning. A myriad of research studies have shown that interactive group learning has positive effects on academic achievement compared to the ever-dominant lecture approach.

For practical application purposes, distinction between the terms, collaborative and cooperative learning, is not necessary. However, to achieve maximum positive outcomes from interactive group learning, this chapter identified a number of elements that should be considered in the design of such group activities. College instructors have a wide range of interactive group activities from which they can choose. Several were discussed in this chapter, ranging from the simple and quick (e.g., think-pair-share) to those that are more elaborate and of longer duration (e.g., team-based learning). Understanding the important role of peer interaction and social relationships in learning is necessary to provide quality education for the 21st century, and integrative group learning techniques offer an effective approach for introducing these concepts into the classroom.

References

Allen, D. E., Duch, B. J., & Groh, S. E. (1996). The power of problem-based learning in teaching introductory science courses. In L. Wilkerson & W. H. Gijselaers (Eds.), *Bringing problem-based learning to higher education: Theory and practice* (New Directions for Teaching and Learning, 68, 43-52). San Francisco, CA: Jossey-Bass.

Angelo, T. A., & Cross, K. P. (1993). *Classroom assessment techniques: A handbook for college teachers* (2nd ed.). San Francisco, CA: Jossey Bass.

Aronson, E. (2013). *Jigsaw classroom. Overview of the technique.* Retrieved from http://www.jigsaw.org/overview.htm

Ashton-Hay, S., & Pillay, H. K. (2010). Case study of collaborative learning in two contexts: What do English language learners gain? In E. Luzzatto & G. DiMarco (Eds.) *Collaborative learning: Methodology, types of interactions and techniques* (Education in a Competitive and Globalizing World series , pp. 341-362). New York, NY: Nova.

Bruffee, K. (1995). Sharing our toys: Cooperative learning versus collaborative learning. *Change, 27*(1), 12-18.

Campbell, D. J. (1988). Task complexity: A review and analysis. *Academy of Management. Review, 13*(1), 40-52.

Carroll, D. W. (2006). Thinking about historical issues: Debates in the history and systems course. *Teaching of Psychology, 33*, 137-140.

Cathey, C. (2007). Power of peer review: an online collaborative learning assignment in social psychology. *Teaching of Psychology, 34*(2), 97-99.

Chickering, A. W., & Gamson, Z. F. (1991). *Applying the seven principles for good practice in undergraduate education.* San Francisco, CA: Jossey-Bass.

Clark, M. C., Nguyen, H. T., Bray, C., & Levine, R. E. (2008). Team-based learning in an undergraduate nursing course. *Nursing Education, 47*(3), 111-117.

Dewey, J. (1963). *Experience and education.* New York, NY: Macmillan.

Dinan, F., & Frydrychowski, V. A. (1995). A team-based learning method for organic chemistry. *Journal of Chemistry Education, 72*(5), 429-431.

Doymus, K. (2008). Teaching chemical equilibrium with the jigsaw technique. *Research in Science Education, 38*, 249-260.

Dunn, D. S. (2000). Letter exchanges on statistics and research methods: Writing, responding, and learning. *Teaching of Psychology, 27*, 128-130.

Edens, K. M. (2000). Preparing problem solvers for the 21st century through problem-based learning. *College Teaching, 48*(2), 55-60.

Engel, C. E. (1991). Not just a method but a way of learning. In D. Boud & G. Feletti (Eds.), *The challenge of problem-based learning* (pp. 23-33). New York, NY: St. Martin's Press.

Epstein Educational Enterprises. (n.d.). *IF-AT.* Retrieved from http://www.epsteineducation.com

Farley, J., Erickson, J. D., & Daly, H. (2005). *Ecological economics: A workbook for problem-based learning.* Washington, DC: Island Press.

Felder, R. M., & Brent, R. (2007). Cooperative learning. In P. A. Mabrouk (Ed.), *Active learning: Models from the analytical sciences* (pp. 34-53). Washington, DC: American Chemical Society.

Fisher, D., Brozo, W. G., Frey, N., & Ivery, G. (2007). *Content area strategies for adolescent literacy.* Columbus, OH: Pearson.

Gagne, R., & Driscoll, M. (1988). *Essentials of learning for instruction* (2nd ed.). Englewood Cliffs, NJ: Prentice-Hall.

Groccia, J. E. (n.d.) *The Alone-Together-Alone (A-T-A) approach.* Unpublished teaching technique.

Gueldenzoph, L. E., & May, G. L. (2002). Collaborative peer evaluation: Best practices for group member assessments. *Business Communication Quarterly, 65*(1), 9-20.

Hall, S. S., & Seery, B. L. (2006). Behind the facts: Helping students evaluate media reports of psychological research. *Teaching of Psychology, 33,* 101-104. Retrieved from http://www.informaworld.com/smpp/content~db=all~content=a785862670

Haidet, P., O'Malley K. J., & Richards, B. (2002). An initial experience with "team learning" in medical education. *Academic Medicine, 77*(1), 40-44.

Hernandez, S. A. (2002). Team-based learning in a marketing principles course: Cooperative structures that facilitate active learning and higher-level thinking. *Journal of Marketing Education, 24*(2), 45-75.

Herreid, C. F. (2011, Winter). Case study teaching. *New Directions for Teaching and Learning, 128,* 31-40.

Herreid, C. F, & DuRei, K. (2007). Intimate debate: The medicinal use of marijuana. *Journal of College Science Teaching, 36,* 10-13.

Hogan, D. M., & Tudge, J. R. H. (1999). Implications of Vygotsky's theory for peer learning. In A. M. O'Donnell & A. King (Eds.), *Cognitive perspectives on peer learning* (pp. 39-65). Mahwah, NJ: Erlbaum.

Johnson, D. W., & Johnson, R. T. (2009). An educational psychology success story: Social interdependence theory and cooperative learning. *Educational Researcher, 38*(5), 365-379. doi: 10.3102/0013189X09339057

Johnson, D. W., Johnson, R. T., & Holubec, E. J. (1991). Revised cooperation in the classroom. In D. W. Johnson., R. T. Johnson, & K. A. Smith, (Eds.), *Active learning: Cooperation in the college classroom* (pp. 1-6). Edina, MN: Interaction Book.

Johnson, D. W., Johnson, R. T., & Smith, K. A. (1991). *Active learning: Cooperation in the college classroom.* Edina, MN: Interaction Book Company.

Jonassen, D. H. (1997). Instructional design model for well-structured and ill-structured problem-solving learning outcomes. *Educational Technology: Research and Development, 45*(1), 65-95.

Karge, B. D., Phillips, K. M., Jessee, T., & McCabe, M. (2011). Effective strategies for engaging adult learners. *Journal of College Teaching & Learning, 8*(12) 53-56.

Keller. F. S. (1968). Good-bye, teacher. *Journal of Applied Behavior Analysis, 1,* 79-89.

Kelly, J. R., & McGrath, J. E. (1985). Effects of time limits and task types on task performance and interaction of four-person groups. *Journal of Personality and Social Psychology, 49,* 395-407.

Kim, S., Phillips, W. R., Pinsky, L., Brock, D., Phillips, K., & Keary, J. (2006). A conceptual framework for developing teaching cases: A review and synthesis of the literature across disciplines. *Medical Education, 40,* 867-876.

Kolmos, A., Fink, F., & Krough, L. (Eds.) (2004). *The Aalborg PBL-model: Progress, diversity and challenges.* Aalborg, Denmark: Aalborg University Press.

Ku, H., Tseng, H. W., & Akarasriworn, C. (2013). Collaboration factors, teamwork satisfaction, and student attitudes toward online collaborative learning. *Computers in Human Behavior 29,* 922-929.

Lai, E. R. (2011). *Collaboration: A literature review.* Retrieved from http://www.pearsonassessments.com/hai/images/tmrs/Collaboration-Review.pdf

Latane, B., Williams, K., & Harkins, S. (1979). Many hands make light the work: The causes and consequences of social loafing. *Journal of Personality and Social Psychology, 37*(6), 822-832.

Levine, J. M., & Moreland, R. L. (1999). Knowledge transmission in work groups: Helping newcomers to succeed. In L. Thompson, J. Levine, & D. Messick (Eds.), *Shared cognition in organizations: The management of knowledge* (pp. 267-296). Mahwah, NJ: Erlbaum.

Lim, B., & Klein, K. J. (2006). Team mental models and team performance: A field study of the effects of team mental model similarity and accuracy. *Journal of Organizational Behavior, 27,* 403-418.

Lundgren, L. (1994). *Cooperative learning in the science classroom.* New York, NY: Glencoe Division of MacMillan/McGraw-Hill.

Lyman, F. T. (1981). The responsive classroom discussion: The inclusion of all students. In A. Anderson (Ed.), *Mainstreaming digest* (pp. 109-113). College Park, MD: University of Maryland Press.

Major, C. H., & Palmer, B. (2001). Assessing the effectiveness of problem-based learning in higher education: Lessons from the literature. *Academic Exchange Quarterly, 5*(1), 4-8.

Matthews, R. S., Cooper, J. L., Davidson, N., & Hawkes, P. (1995). Building bridges between cooperative and collaborative learning, *Change, 27,* 35-40.

Maudsley, G. (1999). Do we all mean the same thing by problem-based learning? A review of the concepts and a formulation of the ground rules. *Academic Medicine, 74,* 178-185.

McInerney, M. J. (2003) Team-based learning enhances long-term retention and critical thinking in an undergraduate microbial physiology course. *Microbiology Education Journal, 4*(1), 3-12.

Mengduo, Q., & Xiaoling, J. (2010). Jigsaw strategy as a cooperative learning technique: Focusing on the language learners. *Chinese Journal of Applied Linguistics, 33*(4), 113-125.

Mercer, N. (2013). The social brain, language, and goal-directed collective thinking: A social conception of cognition and its implications for understanding how we think, teach, and learn. *Educational Psychologist, 48*(3), 148-168.

Mergendoller, J. R., Bellisimo, Y., & Maxwell, N. L. (2000). Comparing problem-based learning and traditional instruction in high school economics. *Journal of Educational Research, 93*(6), 374-383.

Michaelsen, L. K. (2002a). Getting started with team-based learning. In L. K. Michaelsen, A. Bauman Knight, & L. Dee Fink (Eds.), *Team-based learning: A transformative use of small groups* (pp. 27-51).Westport, CT: Praeger.

Michaelsen, L. K., (2002b). Team-based learning in large classes. In C. Stanley & E. Porter (Eds.), *Engaging large classes: Strategies and techniques for college faculty* (pp. 67-83). New York, NY: Anker.

Michaelsen, L. K., & Sweet, M. (2008). The essential elements of team-based learning. *New Directions for Teaching and Learning, 116,* 7-27. doi: 10.1002/tl.330

Michaelsen, L. K., & Sweet, M. (2011). Team-based learning. *New Directions for Teaching and Learning, 128,* 41-51. doi: 10.1002/tl.465

Millis, B. J., & Cottell, P. G., Jr. (1998). *Cooperative learning for higher education faculty,* (American Council on Education, Series on Higher Education). Phoenix, AZ: The Oryx Press.

National Center for Case Study Teaching in Science (NCCSTS). (n.d). *Case collection.* Retrieved from http://sciencecases.lib.buffalo.edu/cs/collection/

O'Connell, R. M. (2011). Adapting team-based learning to early engineering courses. *Proceedings of the Midwest Section Conference of the American Society for Engineering Education.* Retrieved from https://www.asee.org/documents/sections/midwest/2011/ASEE-MIDWEST_0012_013783.pdf

Ommundsen, P. (2001). *Problem-based learning in biology with 20 case examples.* Retrieved from http://capewest.ca/pbl.html

Oxford, R. (1997). Cooperative learning, collaborative learning, and interaction: Three communicative strands in the language classroom. *The Modern Language Journal, 81*(4), 443-456.

Panitz, T. (1999). *Collaborative versus cooperative learning: A comparison of the two concepts which will help us understand the underlying nature of interactive learning.* Retrieved from http://home.capecod.net/~tpanitz/tedsarticles/coopdefinition.htm

Pattanpichet, F. (2011). The effects of using collaborative learning to enhance students' English speaking achievement. *Journal of College Teaching & Learning, 81*(11), 1-10.

Pear, J. J., Schnerch, G. J., Silva, K. M., Svenningsen, L., & Lambert, J. (2011, Winter). Web-based computer-aided personalized system of instruction. *New Directions for Teaching and Learning, 128,* 85-94.

Popescu, F. F., & Maftei, G. (2012). Teaching atomic physics in secondary school with the jigsaw technique. *Romanian Reports in Physics, 64*(4), 1109-1118.

Restad, P., Onion, R., Reynolds, A., & Sweet, M. (2010). *Doing history with team-based learning in a large survey U.S. history course.* Poster presented at the annual meeting of the Team-Based Learning Collaborative, New Orleans, Louisiana.

Roberts C., Lawson, M., Newble, D., Self, A., & Chan, P. (2005). The introduction of large class problem-based learning into an undergraduate medical curriculum: An evaluation. *Med Teach, 27*(6), 527-533.

Roschelle, J., & Teasley, S. D. (1995). The construction of shared knowledge in collaborative problem-solving. In C. E. O'Malley (Ed.), *Computer-supported collaborative learning* (pp. 69-97). Berlin, Germany: Springer-Verlag.

Royal Society of Arts. (2010). *Curriculum and the social brain* (Royal Society of Arts Education seminars). Retrieved from http://www.thersa.org/action-research-centre/learning,-cognition-and-creativity/education/education-seminars-2010/curriculum-and-the-social-brain

San Francisco State University (SFSU). (2011). *Problem based-learning*. Retrieved from http://online.sfsu.edu/rpurser/revised/pages/problem.htm

Schlenker, B. R., & Weigold, M. E (1989). Goals and the self-identification process: Constructing desired identities. In L. A. Pervin (Ed.), *Goal concepts in personality and social psychology* (pp. 243-290). Hillsdale, NJ: Erlbaum.

Sexton, P. C. (1961). *Education and income*. New York, NY: The Viking Press.

Skilton, P. F., Forsyth, D., & White, O. J. (2008). Interdependence and integration learning in student project teams: Do team project assignments achieve what we want them to? *Journal of Marketing Education, 30*, 57-65. doi: 10.1177/0273475307312198

Skinner, B. F. (1968). *The technology of teaching*. New York, NY: Appleton-Century-Crofts.

Slavin, R. (1996). *Education for all*. Exton, PA: Swets & Zeitlinger.

Smith, K. A. (1995). *Cooperative learning: Effective teamwork for engineering classrooms*. Proceedings of 1995 Frontiers in Education Conference, IEEE, Atlanta, GA. Retrieved from http://ieeexplore.ieee.org/xpls/abs_all.jsp?arnumber=483059&tag=1

Smith, K. A. (1996). Cooperative learning: Making "groupwork" work. *New Directions in Teaching and Learning, 67*, 71-82. doi:10.1002/tl.37219966709

Smith, B. L., & MacGregor, J. T. (1992). What is collaborative learning? In A. Goodsell, M. Maher, V. Tinto, B. L. Smith, & J. MacGregor (Eds.), *Collaborative learning: A sourcebook for higher education* (pp. 10-30). State College, PA: National Center on Postsecondary Teaching, Learning, and Assessment.

Speck, B. W. (2003). Fostering collaboration among students in problem-based learning. *New Directions for Teaching and Learning, 95*, 59-65.

Springer, L., Stanne, M. E., & Donovan, S. S., (1999). Effects of small-group learning on undergraduates in science, mathematics, engineering, and technology: A meta-analysis. *Review of Educational Research, 69*(1), 21-51.

Srinivasan, M., Wilkes, M., Stevenson, F., Nguyen, T., & Slavin, S. (2007). Comparing problem-based learning with case-based learning: Effects of a major curricular shift at two institutions. *Academic Medicine, 82*(1), 74-82.

Stanford University. (n.d.). *Example problems*. Retrieved from http://ldt.stanford.edu/~jeepark/jeepark+portfolio/PBL/example2.htm

Stinson, J. E., & Milter, R. G. (n.d.) *Problem-based learning in business education: Curriculum design and implementation issues*. Retrieved from http://www.ouwb.ohiou.edu/stinson/PBL.html

Terenzini, P., Cabrera, A., Colbeck, C., Parente, J., & Bjorklund, S. (2001) Collaborative learning vs. lecture/discussion: Students' reported learning gains. *Journal of Engineering Education, 90*(1), 123-130.

Tomcho, T. J., & Foels, R. (2012). Meta-analysis of group learning activities: Empirically based teaching recommendations. *Teaching of Psychology, 39*, 159-169.

Vygotsky, L. (1978). *Mind in society: The developmental of higher psychological process.* Cambridge, MA: Harvard University Press.

Wheelan, S. A. (2009). Group size, group development, and group productivity. *Small Group Research, 40,* 247-262. doi:10.1177/1046496408328703

Wheelan, S. A., Davidson, B., & Tilin, F. (2003). Group development across time: Reality or illusion? *Small Group Research, 34,* 223-245.

Williams, B. A. (2001). Introductory physics: A problem-based model. In B. J. Duch, S. E. Groh, & D. E. Allen (Eds.), *The power of problem-based learning* (p. 265). Sterling, VA: Stylus.

Wilson, W. R., (1982). *The use of permanent learning groups in teaching introductory accounting* (Unpublished doctoral dissertation). Norman, OK: University of Oklahoma.

Yalom, I. D., & Leszcz, M. (2005). *The theory and practice of group psychotherapy* (5th ed.) New York, NY: Basic Books.

Chapter 8
Engaging Students in Online Environments

Amy Collier

"I never teach my pupils, I only attempt to provide the conditions in which they can learn."
– Albert Einstein

Einstein's influential words about teaching resonate with many instructors' experiences. Whether teaching an online introductory class in physics or a capstone course in anthropology, instructors often say their greatest joys come from moments when students take advantage of the class environment to seize ownership of their learning. While some of these moments may happen by chance—an alignment of a developmental moment in a student's life and a responsive teacher—there is evidence that classes can be designed for this kind of student-centered learning, known as *active learning* (Bonwell & Eison, 1991). However, for instructors of online and *blended courses* (having some online elements), designing online environments for active learning can be a daunting task. This chapter provides support for instructors of these courses by outlining evidence-supported approaches for engaging students via active online learning.

Bonwell and Eison (1991) defined active learning as students doing things in class and reflecting on their experiences. In passive classrooms, the teacher is the primary actor, imparting information to students, asking and answering questions, and testing students' retrieval of information (Petress, 2008). In the active-learning classroom, students are the primary actors, engaging in meaningful activities and taking ownership of their learning.

Research suggests that passive or traditional didactic teaching (i.e., lecturing) is insufficient to foster ownership and engagement from students (Donovan, Bransford, & Pellegrino, 1999; Johnson, Johnson, & Smith, 1991). Active learning, however, is believed to promote engagement that positively shapes what students learn, how well they learn it, and their attitudes toward learning. The goal of active learning is to move students toward a deeper understanding of materials and the ability to engage in higher-order thinking skills (Bonwell & Eison, 1991), while keeping them motivated (Barkley, 2010). Active learning also positively impacts the classroom environment and community because of its emphasis on student-to-student interaction (Yazedjian & Kolkhorst, 2007).

While active learning can refer to a particular teaching and learning strategy, it is more commonly used as an umbrella term under which more specific strategies fall (Prince, 2004). The active-learning umbrella includes collaborative learning, inquiry-based learning, flipped classes, and a host of other teaching and learning approaches. Several of these active-learning practices will be explained in this chapter. Though active-learning methods differ, they have five core commonalities: (a) students' active participation in learning beyond didactic processes; (b) a focus on the development of skills, not just retention of information; (c) development of higher-order thinking skills; (d) student engagement in activities that promote deeper student learning; and (e) reflection and metacognitive (i.e., thinking and learning about learning) skills (Bonwell & Eison, 1991).

These five core elements of active learning may be easy to spot in a face-to-face class, but how are they fostered online? Due to a perceived lack of social and cultural cues people use to connect to each other, online environments are often seen as impersonal. Despite this, the online environment is well suited to active learning because it is unhindered by the physical constraints that sometime impede active-learning activities in a traditional classroom. Today's students are also much more connected online than in the past, allowing for active learning to take place in many contexts and via many devices. Further, with a little effort, most online environments can shift power from the teacher to the student and provide a setting in which students are taking the lead in their learning. Hence, online learning environments can be designed to foster active student learning by leveraging the access, interactivity, connection, and user agency these environments provide.

To effectively use active learning online, instructors must carefully plan their strategies and design for the online environment. This chapter will outline research-supported approaches to engaging students online and provide examples from instructors at several educational institutions. These methods will cover (a) learner-content engagement, (b) learner-instructor engagement, (c) learner-learner engagement, and (d) evolving applications for online learning. The first three topics are lenses, first proposed in Moore's (1989) exploration of online interactions, and are not intended to be rigid categorizations but rather useful frameworks through which approaches can be understood. The final section will introduce *flipped classrooms* (i.e., content delivery happens outside the classroom while guided practice and concept engagement happen within the classroom), which are gaining in popularity in higher education today and provide a unique approach to classroom structure using online elements. A resources page listing web addresses of a variety of online tools is provided at the end of this chapter.

Learner-Content Engagement

Active-learning proponents often refer to content delivery in a course as passive, with students receiving content via lecture or textbooks. Even online content is seen as passive, evoking images of learners staring blankly at screens or receiving online content while multitasking with more engaging media. Within that mindset, discussing learner-content engagement might seem anathema.

In active learning, however, the goal is to create an environment where students' interaction with content is dynamic and leads to deeper engagement with course topics. Simulations, interactive content, and games can help make content more engaging for students but can be difficult and time-consuming to produce. In the next sections, strategies for fostering student interaction with content, without requiring heavy time or skill commitments, will be explained.

Driving Content Engagement Through Questions

Inquiry-based learning is a way of engaging students with content by asking them to find and make sense of content, rather than expecting it to be delivered to them. This approach, which can be used in face-to-face and online classes, begins with a broad question, often ill-defined and open-ended, and provides scaffolding for students' exploration of course content to answer that question (Musawi, Asan, Abdelraheem, & Osmans, 2012). Inquiry has been shown to help students make gains in conceptual understanding and improve process and literacy skills associated with course topics (Brickman, Gormally, Armstrong, & Haller, 2009).

This type of learning works in online learning environments because of the important role web resources and networked connections can play in inquiry. However, inquiry-based learning does require substantial instructor involvement, such as giving feedback to teams, helping students get unstuck when they reach dead-ends, and sprinkling helpful assessments throughout the process to assist teams in monitoring and adjusting their progress (Miller, 2008). These tasks are somewhat harder to do online because of the interpersonal distance that many students and instructors experience. Instructors who plan to use inquiry learning in their online classes should prepare instructor-facilitated feedback and scaffolding activities to support student inquiry teams, such as an activity to teach students how to use library resources in their inquiry process.

The inquiry process begins with a trigger to launch students' exploration of a topic (Garrison, Anderson, & Archer, 2001). Miller (2008) recommended using a video to set up the area for exploration. Other media triggers could include sound clips, archival footage, or primary source documents. Regardless of the format, triggers should elicit multiple questions that spark students' curiosity and prompt them to seek the best sources of evidence to support their hypotheses. Figure 8.1 offers a list of possible inquiry questions across various disciplines.

In online courses, students doing inquiry learning may be expected to join a discussion with their teammates to talk about what they think is happening or will happen. From there, the teams can begin researching and collecting ideas to formulate hypotheses for the problem presented. This part of the inquiry process is known as *exploration*. Here, students can leverage the expansive networks of information and people available on the Internet. At the conclusion of their explorations, teams are expected to present a product, a solution, or a response to the inquiry. While this interaction could happen asynchronously, via a discussion forum or similar tools, synchronous tools may be best for postinquiry discussions, allowing students and instructors to give immediate responses and feedback to the teams.

Example: Inquiry Learning

Stanford University instructor Anne Friedlander took a creative approach to inquiry learning in her Environmental Physiology course. She and a teaching assistant created *Where Is Corey Now?* videos featuring the teaching assistant in a variety of physiologically stressful environments (e.g., cold climate or high altitude)

Social sciences	How would government/social/economic responses have been different if Hurricane Katrina had struck New Orleans before 9/11? How are responses to hurricanes different today (post Katrina)?
Natural sciences	What influences the percentage of our brain that we use? What would happen if all coral disappeared from the oceans? How much would anthropogenic greenhouse gases need to be reduced to reverse the global warming trend?
Humanities	How would society change if everyone suddenly lost the sense of sight? The sense of touch?
Computer sciences and engineering	Where does our school's library store its digital archives? How can the efficiency of wind turbines be improved?

Figure 8.1. Inquiry questions across various disciplines.

and captured data from his body's responses to the conditions. Rather than fully explaining in the video what was happening to Corey's body, Friedlander pointed to the data, noting important changes, enigmas, and concerns that students should consider. Students watched the videos online before class and then, as part of in-class group work, investigated what was happening to Corey's body. Friedlander and her teaching assistants moved around the groups to answer questions, seed ideas, or help find the right resources to investigate. In some face-to-face class sessions, Friedlander reproduced the conditions from Corey's videos and allowed students to experience those conditions themselves. At the end of each session, she led a discussion among the teams about what they found, where they went astray, and takeaways from the inquiry (personal communication, August 14, 2013).

Creating Online Concept Maps

Concept mapping is a method of visually outlining relationships between concepts in a course or subconcepts within a topic (Figure 8.2). When students make these connections between course concepts, they improve their ability to recall and understand those topics (Karpicke & Grimaldi, 2012). Further, concept maps help students engage in synthesis and evaluation of course concepts, potentially deepening their understanding (Angelo & Cross, 1993). These visual displays may also be used in combination with inquiry approaches to help learners organize their findings (Musawi et al., 2012). Students' concept maps give instructors a good sense of the learner's conceptual schemata and can provide opportunities to address misconceptions or missing connections (Angelo & Cross, 1993).

The rise of social web technologies has brought a suite of tools that can be used for individual or group-based concept mapping. Online mind mapping tools, such as MindMeister, allow students to create and share concept maps; some tools (e.g., Prezi Meeting) let multiple students collaboratively and synchronously build concept maps (Figure 8.2). For example, students can begin with a shared presentation space and synchronously add concepts, connect ideas using arrows, and highlight relationships with circles and other visual tools. While the tool sets for online concept mapping are evolving, using tools for engaging students with content remains an effective and easy-to-implement practice.

Simulations and Games

Interactive content can offer fun and engaging opportunities for students to connect with a subject. However, most instructors do not have the time and resources needed to create effective games, simulations, and other forms of interactive content. Rather than focusing on its creation, instructors may look to reuse interactive tools and strategies developed by other faculty or open courseware initiatives, such as MIT's Open Courseware. The University of Colorado at Boulder developed a reputable series of physics simulations, known as PhET, that teach concepts ranging from molarity to plate tectonics. Learning object repositories, such as MERLOT, may also offer simulations and games for a wide range of disciplines.

Learner-Instructor Engagement

Though active-learning models call for greater student participation in the learning process, they do not propose a reduction in faculty engagement. Rather, active learning requires substantial commitment and engagement from both students and instructors (Barkley, 2010). Active learning shifts the role of the instructor to expert facilitator and guide. This approach emphasizes the importance of creating a space for student practice, allowing students the freedom to fail, and provides timely, contextual, rich, and meaningful feedback to enhance learning.

Learner-instructor interaction can be difficult in online courses, particularly large online courses, and online instructors often replace learner-instructor engagement demands (e.g., providing rich feedback, responding to inquiries, being available for student questions) with more learner-content interaction (Anderson, 2003). However, learner-instructor engagement is likely to have the most perceived value to the students in both face-to-face and online environments (Anderson, 2003). For this reason, instructors should look for technologies that help them interact with students in timely, effective, and efficient ways. The next two sections recommend strategies and tools for instructor-learner engagement.

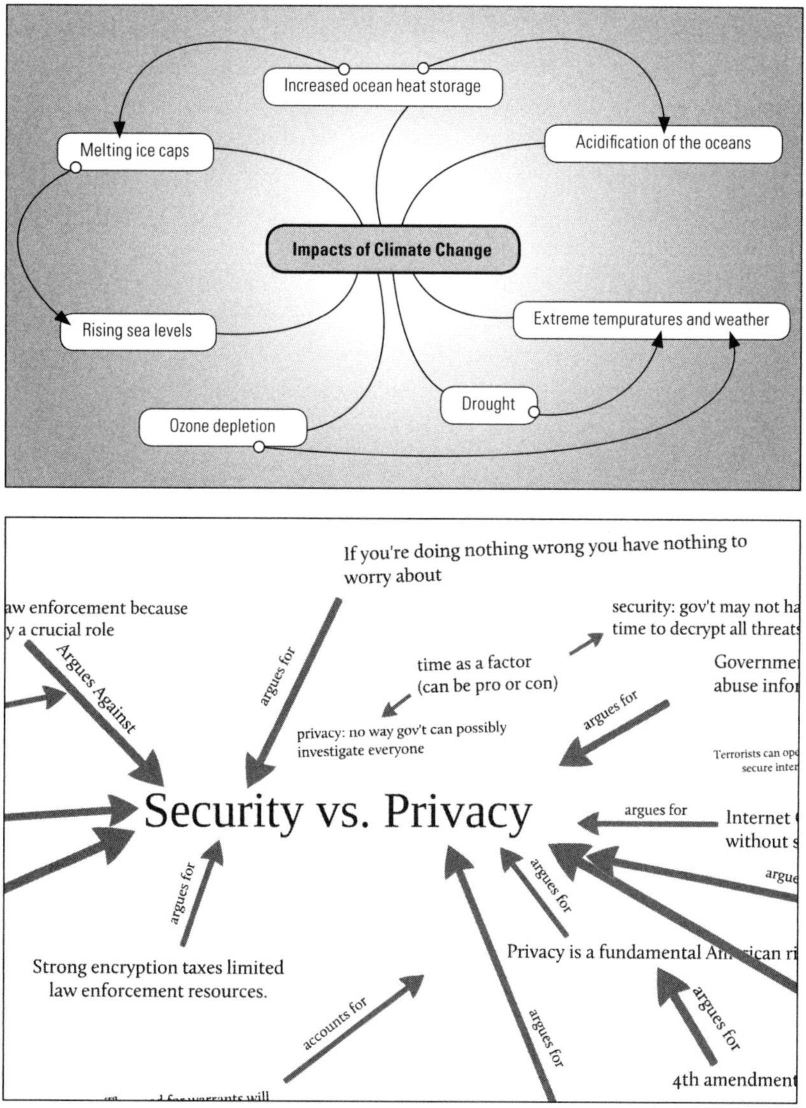

Figure 8.2. Two examples of online concept mapping: Mindmeister and Prezi. Bottom image adapted from "*In-Class Collaborative Debate Mapping With Prezi Meeting*" by D. Bruff, Agile Learning Blog, November 30, 2010. Copyright 2014 by Agile Learning. Reprinted with permission.

Formative Assessment and Feedback

Formative assessment is intended to help students develop their understanding of course topics by providing a mechanism for immediate and useful feedback. *Formative feedback* assists students in making progress in their learning by helping them reflect on and improve their learning processes. Svinicki and McKeachie (2011) noted, to be effective, feedback should be specific, contextualized, forward-looking, timely, and transferable.

Timely formative feedback focuses on students' learning processes, allowing them to make adjustments to what they are doing in a course to improve their outcomes. In online and blended learning, formative feedback can also help convey a sense of immediacy that may be less obvious in an online environment. Fostering immediacy, particularly in a fully online course, can aid in overcoming feelings of distance between instructors and students (Shackelford & Maxwell, 2012; Thweatt & McCroskey, 1996).

Examples of formative feedback are short, embedded online quizzes sprinkled throughout the environment to give students a chance for self-assessment, self-reflection, and instructor feedback. Online learning platforms, such as Canvas or Blackboard, provide functionality for instructors to create low-stakes objective quizzes students can take multiple times and that have built-in feedback to help them learn from mistakes and reflect on correct answers. Paired with immediate feedback, frequent online low-stakes quizzes have been shown to improve students' performance in courses (Johnson & Kiviniemi, 2009).

Formative feedback is also important for students' written or creative work. Grading written assignments and providing extensive feedback is time-consuming, and students often do not use the instructors' comments to improve their work. In addition, feedback on written work may arrive too late for action, and this can impact online students' success in a course. To combat feedback delays, some instructors record audio and/or video feedback on students' work, which can be done for individuals, groups, or the entire class (see example on the Resources page at the end of this chapter). Audio or video feedback may provide more thorough and contextual feedback to students while allowing students to pause and replay the feedback as needed (Pan et al., 2012).

Feedback screencasts are easy to produce using free or low-cost software, such as Jing or Camtasia, and can be distributed to students via e-mail or in students' online dropboxes. This technology allows instructors to provide timely contextual feedback on students' written and creative works.

Similarly, instructors may offer audio and video feedback to small groups or the entire class. These types of feedback can help students feel engaged with the instructor, whether in a fully online or blended environment, and monitor and adjust their learning processes throughout a course. For example, at the end of each section of an online course, an instructor might create a short video summarizing important points, addressing common misconceptions, or preparing students for upcoming topics. Small groups may benefit from a video of the instructor reviewing their group work and group processes, and perhaps sharing a message of encouragement. These feedback media can be recorded using smartphone-based applications, inexpensive web cameras attached to computers, or consumer-grade video cameras.

Example: Assignment-Based Feedback to Online Students

In the author's online course at Texas Wesleyan University, video was used to provide feedback on assignments. The feedback was not specific to any one student; rather, it broadly addressed how the class performed related to the goals for assignments. These videos dealt with misconceptions, questions, and concerns the students expressed; sometimes the videos provided encouragement or introductions for upcoming modules. The instructor-made videos (IMVs) provided conceptual scaffolding for students (Pan et al., 2012) and were created using a small digital USB camera (i.e., Flip Cam) and a consumer video editing software tool (i.e., iMovie). The IMVs were distributed via YouTube and embedded in the announcements section of the online courses. An example of an IMV is available on the resources page at the end of this chapter.

Synchronous Technologies to Connect Instructors and Students

Synchronous discussion tools may include text-based chat, document and desktop sharing, breakout chat sessions, virtual whiteboards, sketchpads or mind maps, and recording capabilities. Text-based synchronous technologies, such as chat rooms and Twitter, are used by instructors for communicating and sharing resources with students in real time. Synchronous technologies may foster immediacy and presence in online and blended courses, especially when those technologies include live video, as with Google Hangouts or Skype. Instructors can use synchronous communication tools to reduce instructor-student interpersonal distance and provide students with more opportunities for feedback and mentoring.

Virtual classrooms and chats have been part of learning management systems (LMS) for decades, and instructors have used these tools to hold virtual office hours, real-time discussions, live icebreaker activities, and live lectures. On-campus technology experts often provide support for these tools, which exist within a familiar course environment. The key limitation of LMS-based tools is they are closed to people and networks outside of the university, restricting possible collaborations, wider discussions, and participation by guest speakers. In addition, tools that are outside of the LMS evolve more quickly than those within the system because of the broader consumer base for non-LMS tools. Instructors should investigate the pros and cons of working with LMS and non-LMS tools, such as Google Hangouts, and determine which fit best with their instructional goals.

Google Hangouts have grown in popularity among educators for the toolsets they provide for synchronous discussion, such as team meetings where sharing features allow students to collaborate on documents and presentations. Hangouts enlarge the video feed of the person speaking, making them good online spaces for debates, interviews, and brainstorming activities. Some instructors use the recording capabilities of Hangouts to invite guest speakers to a live interview and stream the recording of the interview on YouTube. Hangouts also include text-based chat so students can take notes or discuss ideas in text while video-based discussions are occurring.

Learner-Learner Engagement

Perhaps the greatest evolutions in teaching, resulting from affordances of social technologies, are in the area of learner-to-learner engagement. Social technologies link learners to a global audience and foster more meaningful interactions among learners within the same class. Meaningful interactions are an essential part of active learning—both online and in face-to-face classes—and they must be carefully cultivated. Research evidence points to the incomparable value of peer-to-peer interactions for learning, if those peer interactions are structured for discussion, questioning, explanation, and feedback (Boyle & Nicol, 2003). Some social technologies may even act as social glue for online or blended learners, helping them to feel as though they belong to a class even though they may not always connect to other learners face-to-face (Dorum, Bartle, & Pennington, 2010).

Social technologies present great opportunities and challenges for peer-to-peer interactions. For example, social media are used by many students for non-academic purposes and, therefore, are familiar and accessible to them. However, these technologies are also sources of distraction, and some students may struggle to understand how they can be used for learning. Instructors should leverage the networked power of learner-to-learner engagement technologies but keep students focused on course goals by clearly stating expectations and outcomes for the use of social technologies. The next sections present specific strategies and tools for learner-learner engagement.

Online Peer Review and Feedback

Peer review (see Chapter 9 for more information on assessment) is an active-learning technique that involves students' analyzing and evaluating other students' work (Odom, Glenn, Sanner, & Cannella, 2009). With peer review, students learn how to provide actionable feedback on work products while developing metacognitive skills that help them evaluate and improve their own work. Peer review is difficult to effectively facilitate in the face-to-face classroom, and perhaps even more so online. However, new online tools for peer review, and a renewed interest in large-scale review, such as in massive open online courses (MOOCS), have provided insights into improving online peer assessment.

Rubrics are an essential ingredient for successful peer review, outlining expectations for student work and assigning numeric or categorical values to describe how well that work meets expectations. For online peer review, rubrics must feature clear statements of expectations so students can make sense of them with less instructor oversight (Kulkarni & Klemmer, 2012). Language on the rubrics should be free of jargon and not assume that students understand technical terminology or the rationale behind the assignment criteria.

Though students may be able to accurately evaluate each other's work using rubrics, many struggle to provide actionable feedback other learners can use. To help, instructors can scaffold feedback in the online environment by providing prompts that can spark useful feedback exchanges among students. Klemmer and Kulkarni (2012) called these prompts *fortune cookie feedback* (Figure 8.3), which are snippets of feedback based on common errors and possible ameliorative actions for a given assignment. These snippets are provided to students while they are reviewing others' work to seed appropriate qualitative feedback. An example of fortune cookie feedback in a history class may be, "Cite primary sources, instead of secondary sources, to add credibility to your arguments." A student can copy the fortune cookie feedback into a text box and supplement it with additional feedback text. This approach has been shown to improve the quantity and quality of feedback learners provide to each other (Klemmer & Kulkarni, 2012).

Discussion forums are perhaps the simplest tools for peer review, allowing students to post their work to a discussion thread and letting others provide feedback in subsequent threaded responses. Some discussion forums can have restricted membership so that only students in an assigned group can see and review each other's work. Online document services, like Dropbox, Box, or Google Docs, can also be used for peer assessment. Students can upload their work to shared folders with each of those services and provide in-document feedback to other students.

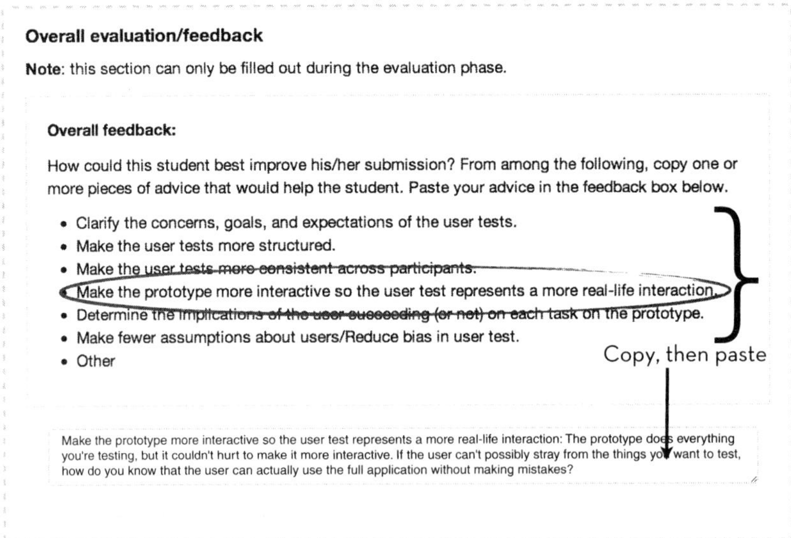

Figure 8.3. Fortune cookie feedback. Adapted from "Peer and Self Assessment in Massive Online Courses," by C. Kulkarni et al., 2013, *ACM Transactions on Human-Computer Interaction, 20*(6), p.18. Copyright 2013 by ACM. Reprinted with permission.

Newer online learning platforms, such as Coursera and OpenEdX, have built-in peer review systems for courses. These systems are sophisticated, facilitating calibrated peer review, but may be more difficult for students to use.

Example: Online Peer Review

Scott Klemmer, a professor at the University of California-San Diego, taught a public online course on Human-Computer Interaction using calibrated peer review to assess students' work (Kulkarni & Klemmer, 2012). Calibrated peer review requires students to assess prewritten and graded texts, using the rubric for the assignment, before they can review other students' work (Kulkarni & Klemmer, 2012). If a student's review of the prewritten text meets standards, he or she can begin reviewing other students' work. In Klemmer's class, students submitted design assignments to the platform's peer assessment system and began the calibrated review process. Students who successfully passed the calibration process then reviewed the work of five other students. In addition to providing a numeric grade, students were encouraged to give each other qualitative feedback, starting with the fortune cookie prompts (Figure 8.3; Klemmer & Kulkarni, 2012). To help students improve the quality of their work, they were shown examples from papers that were scored slightly higher than their own. Klemmer and Kulkarni (2012) found that students who were shown somewhat better papers as examples improved their performance compared to students who were shown the highest scoring papers as examples.

Shared Curation and Discussion of Course Content

Online curation is the organizing, tagging, and sharing of web content with a network of online users. Technologies for online social curation, such as Pinterest and Tumblr, have made their way into classrooms and universities. Students may use these tools and websites to collect and display resources for a course. Many of these technologies also allow students to build discussions around curated content, providing embedded conversations for students to make sense of the content.

These visual curation tools may be particularly useful in disciplines in which imagery and media are important parts of course content. For example, Pinterest displays content with large images to an individual or shared themed gallery, called a *pin board*. In a class on Asian and Indonesian cultures, students might post links and images to a shared pin board labeled Javanese Clothing. Students can comment on and reshare pins on the board. For instance, at Keene State College in New Hampshire, students in a Design for Performing Arts course shared images of design ideas with explanatory text in the comments for each pin (Educause Learning Initiative, 2007).

Another social curation site, Storify, allows students to collect and display various media to form a sequenced narrative. For example, students in a class on Democratic Development might aggregate media, including images, videos, and Tweets, into a shared narrative about events in emerging democracies or in nondemocratic nations.

Where social curation tools like Pinterest and Storify use text-based discussion around curated content, Voicethread and Flipgrid facilitate audio and video discussion around this content. Both services allow instructors and students to upload media and then record audio or video responses to those media. Pacansky-Brock (2009) shared an example of a Voicethread assignment in which students were required to create a gallery of photos taken by a local photographer and layer those photos with an audio interview with the photographer. Once the galleries were shared with the class, other students could add audio and video comments to them. Pacansky-Brock noted that, in classes where she used Voicethread, 81% of her students said that interacting with other students on Voicethread increased their sense of community in the class.

Online Social Connections

Social networking technologies are increasingly pervasive among college-aged learners. A 2012 report by the Pew Research Center found that 67% of Internet users access social networking sites, with this number rising to 83% for users between the ages of 18 and 29 (Duggan & Brenner, 2012). Because of their widespread use, social networking technologies may afford the greatest opportunities for community building among learners in a course; however, for effective learning, these technologies may also require the greatest *communal scaffolding*—the process of helping online students bridge interpersonal distance (Woods & Ebersole, 2002). This scaffolding involves setting clear expectations for how learners should interact (*netiquette*), allowing learners to write and discuss guidelines for interacting on those sites, and modeling or mentoring from the instructor.

Social technologies provide students with access to a large, diverse, and information-rich distributed network of people. In a digital storytelling class (ds106) at the University of Mary Washington, students connect to each other and to a broad network of people online through the course's blog, web-based radio station (ds106 Radio), and crowd-sourced assignments database (DS106, n.d.). Learners can also network with each other and peers outside the classroom via collaborative-editing websites, like wikis or Google Sites, and via community sites, like Google Plus and Facebook. Each social networking site offers opportunities for learners to connect, but the choice of which sites to use should be made carefully. Instructors must consider how much control and access they want to give learners in online social environments and help students learn about protecting their privacy, appropriate and inappropriate sharing of personal information, and acquiring other social media literacy skills.

Some instructors use Twitter to help students connect to other learners inside and outside of the classroom. Twitter streams provide more immediate interaction opportunities for students than discussion forums and can link students to experts, practitioners, and other learners in their fields. Instructors may encourage students to follow experts or practitioners via Twitter and share those professional insights with other classmates. For example, a geology instructor may encourage students to follow the Curiosity rover as it tweets from the surface of Mars. In addition, an instructor may use Twitter as a discussion forum, asking students to respond to questions and interact with other students' responses in real time. Twitter might also be used to help online students develop a sense of belonging by sharing small bits of information about their personal or academic lives.

Evolving Applications for Active Online Learning

This chapter has outlined tools and approaches for engaging students in online active learning. As online technologies evolve, instructors may find new approaches to engage their students or help them connect more deeply with course content and/or other students. One such emerging model, the *flipped classroom*, is described in detail in this section.

Flipped Classes: Taking Content Outside the Classroom

In a traditional lecture-based course, class time is used for content transmission and understanding activities, such as lecture, while time outside of class is used for application and synthesis activities (e.g., homework and group work). The flipped class aims to invert the traditional model by moving content transmission activities outside of class time and moving higher-order cognitive tasks into the classroom. This model of blended learning is designed to make the most out of in-class interactions, when students and instructors are in the same room and can provide real-time feedback and support to each other.

The flipped class model has grown in popularity since its inception in the late 1990s, as an outgrowth of Mazur's (1997) peer instruction model, which emphasized peer-to-peer learning interwoven with direct instruction to help students better understand and retain course concepts. In 2000, Lage, Platt, and Treglia introduced the term *inverted class* to refer to their approach to fostering more student engagement; later that year, Baker (2000) coined *flipped class*, which is now widely used in education circles. The flipped class model is enjoying a surge in interest because of growing global interest in blended and online learning.

Another reason for growing interest in the flipped model is the availability of easy-to-use consumer-grade video capture and editing software for recording content. With screencasting software, like Camtasia, instructors can very quickly assemble short videos for students to watch before class. The length of video varies greatly between topics and between instructors; however, creating shorter and more focused videos (between 7-20 minutes) may help with student attention and with easier editing of video content. To check students' conceptual understanding and/or provide feedback, some host platforms allow quizzes to be embedded within a video or offer tools for self-evaluation immediately after a video.

One difficulty in implementing a flipped class involves planning what to do with in-class time. Instructors have used in-class time for team-based learning and peer learning activities, such as workshopping each other's papers (e.g., editing, giving feedback, discussing argumentation) or working in groups to solve problems.

Using results from quizzes embedded in videos, or through in-class discussions, instructors may find that students need deeper dives into difficult concepts or, perhaps, to backtrack to core concepts they have misunderstood. Instructors may even use class time to get out of the classroom, offering field trips, experiential- and service-learning, community- or industry-based projects, and labs.

Example: Flipping a Humanities Class

In 2011, Richard Newton, a professor at Cal Poly Pomona, began flipping his class on Ethnicity, Gender, and Religion to foster deeper and more active learning among his students (Barnett, 2013). Before flipping his class, his students struggled to delve deeply into topics because they had not developed skills for analysis and argumentation. Newton began recording short screencasts on those topics to help students better prepare for class. He used screencasting software, such as Doceri or Educreations, on his tablet device to record these screencasts and distributed them to students before class via YouTube (see example on resources page). When his students arrived prepared, Newton used class time for more in-depth activities. In one class, for example, he posed the question: Does hip hop promote or hinder efforts toward gender equality? Students worked in groups to write thesis statements in response to the question and then spent the remainder of the class time arguing for or against other groups' statements (Barnett, 2013).

Conclusion

Instructors may find support for learning about and adopting new active online learning techniques at their universities' centers for teaching and learning or academic technology offices. Or, they may discover new strategies by connecting with online communities of practice via blogs, Twitter, and open online courses designed for educators. Online publications by EdSurge and the Educause Learning Initiative can also guide instructors' use of emerging technologies for active online learning.

Online environments can be spaces for active student learning. With careful planning and design of online environments, instructors can help create conditions where students can make the most of their learning, seize ownership of their process, and embark on a journey of continuos lifelong learning.

Resources

Concept Mapping Tools

Mindmeister: http://www.mindmeister.com/
Bubbl.us: https://bubbl.us/
Prezi Meeting: http://prezi.com/collaborate/

Open Courseware

MIT OpenCourseware: http://ocw.mit.edu/
PhET: http://phet.colorado.edu/
MERLOT: http://www.merlot.org/

Online Platforms

Blackboard: http://www.blackboard.com/
Canvas.net: https://www.canvas.net/
Coursera: https://www.coursera.org/
EdX: http://mooc.org

Online Resource Publications

EdSurge: https://www.edsurge.com/
Educause Learning Initiative: http://www.educause.edu/eli

Screencasting

Jing: http://www.techsmith.com/jing.html
Camtasia: http://www.techsmith.com/camtasia.html
iMovie: http://www.apple.com/ilife/imovie/
Example: IMV: http://www.youtube.com/watch?v=E-H1eGjFSPU (Used with author's permission)
Doceri: http:// http://doceri.com/
Educreations: http://www.educreations.com/

Synchronous Communication

Google Hangouts: http://www.google.com/+/learnmore/hangouts/
Twitter: https://twitter.com/
Skype: http://skype.com

Social Tools

Pinterest: http://pinterest.com/
Facebook: http://facebook.com
Tumblr: https://www.tumblr.com/
Storify: http://storify.com/
Voicethread: http://voicethread.com/
Flipgrid: http://flipgrid.com/info/
Google Sites: http://sites.google.com

Document Storage, Sharing, and Collaboration Tools

Dropbox: http://dropbox.com
Box: http://box.com
Google Docs: http://docs.google.com/

References

Anderson, T. (2003). Getting the mix right again: An updated and theoretical rationale for interaction. *International Review of Research in Open and Distance Learning, 4*(2), 1-15.

Angelo, T. A., & Cross, K. P. (1993). *Classroom assessment techniques* (2nd ed.). San Francisco, CA: Jossey-Bass.

Baker , J. W. (2000). *The classroom flip: Using web course management tools to become the guide by the side.* Paper presented at the 11th International Conference on College Teaching and Learning, Jacksonville, FL.

Barkley, E. (2010). *Student engagement techniques: A handbook for college faculty.* San Francisco, CA: Jossey-Bass.

Barnett, B. (2013). Flipping the higher ed humanities classroom: Teaching critical thinking at Cal Poly Pomona. *Freedom to Teach: The Doceri blog.* Retrieved from http://doceri.com/blog/2013/04/flipping-the-higher-ed-humanities-classroom-teaching-critical-thinking-at-cal-poly-pomona/#sthash.yh7pHcKU.dpuf

Bonwell, C. C., & Eison, J. A. (1991). *Active learning: Creating excitement in the classroom* (ASHE-ERIC Higher Education Report No. 1). Washington, DC: ASHE.

Boyle, J. T., & Nicol, D. J. (2003). Using classroom communication systems to support interaction and discussion in large class settings. *Research in Learning Technology, 11*(3), 43-57.

Brickman, P., Gormally, C., Armstrong, N., & Hallar, B. (2009). Effects of inquiry-based learning on students' science literacy skills and confidence. *International Journal for the Scholarship of Teaching and Learning,* 3(2), 1-22.

Bruff, D. (2010, November 30). In-class collaborative debate mapping with prezi meeting. *Agile Learning Blog.* Retrieved from http://derekbruff.org/?p=595

Donovan, M. S., Bransford, J. D., & Pellegrino, J. W. (Eds.). (1999). *How people learn: Bridging research and practice.* Washington, DC: National Academies Press.

Dorum, K., Bartle, C., & Pennington, M. (2010). The effect of online social networking on facilitating sense of belonging among university students living off campus. In *Proceedings of World Conference on Educational Multimedia, Hypermedia and Telecommunications 2010* (pp. 529-535). Chesapeake, VA: AACE.

DS106. (n.d.). *About DS106.* Retrieved from http://ds106.us/about

Duggan, M., & Brenner, J. (2012). *The demographics of social media users – 2012* (The Pew Research Center report). Retrieved from http://www.pewinternet.org/~/media//Files/Reports/2013/PIP_SocialMediaUsers.pdf

Educause Learning Initiative. (2007). *7 things you should know about social content curation.* Retrieved from: http://net.educause.edu/ir/library/pdf/ELI7089.pdf

Garrison, D. R., Anderson, T., & Archer, W. (2001). Critical thinking, cognitive presence, and computer conferencing in distance education. *American Journal of Distance Education, 15*(1), 7-23.

Johnson, D. W., Johnson, R. T., & Smith, K. A. (1991). *Active learning: Cooperation in the college classroom.* Edina, MN: Interaction.

Johnson, B. C., & Kiviniemi, M. T. (2009). The effect of online chapter quizzes on exam performance in an undergraduate social psychology course. *Teach Psychology, 36*(1), 33-37.

Karpicke, J. D., & Grimaldi, P. (2012). Retrieval-based learning: A perspective for enhancing meaningful learning. *Educational Psychology Review, 24*, 401-418.

Klemmer, S., & Kulkarni, C. (2012). *Scaling studio critique.* Presentation at MIT CSAIL. Retrieved from http://hci.stanford.edu/publications/2012/2012-10-10-StudioCritiqueMIT.pdf

Kulkarni, C., & Klemmer, S. (2012). *Learning design wisdom by augmenting physical studio critique with online self-assessment* (Stanford University HCI Group Technical Report). Retrieved from http://hci.stanford.edu/publications/2012/SelfAssessmentInDesignSpring2012TR.pdf

Kulkarni, C., Wei, K. P., Le, H., Chia, D., Papadopoulos, K., Cheng, J., Koller, D., & Klemmer, S. R. (2013). Peer and self assessment in massive online courses. *ACM Transactions on Human-Computer Interaction, 20*(6), 1-31. Retrieved from http://dl.acm.org/citation.cfm?doid=2562181.2505057

Lage, M., Platt, G., & Treglia, M. (2000). Inverting the classroom: A gateway to creating an inclusive learning environment. *The Journal of Economic Education, 31*(1), 30-43.

Mazur, E. (1997). *Peer instruction: A user's manual.* Upper Saddle River, NJ: Prentice Hall.

Moore, M. G. (1989). Three types of interaction. *The American Journal of Distance Education, 3*(2), 1-6.

Miller, K. (2008). Teaching science methods online: Myths about inquiry-based online learning. *Science Educator, 17*(2), 80-86.

Musawi, A. A., Asan, A., Abdelraheem, A., & Osmans, M. (2012). A case of web-based inquiry learning model using learning objects. *The Turkish Online Journal of Educational Technology, 11*(1), 1-9.

Odom, S., Glenn, B., Sanner, S., & Cannella, K. (2009). Group peer review as an active learning strategy in a research course. *International Journal of Teaching and Learning in Higher Education, 21,* 108-117.

Pacansky-Brock, M. (2009). *Improved deep learning with voicethread.* Retrieved from http://www.slideshare.net/brocansky/vt-for-deeplearningflipped

Pan, G., Sen, S. Starrett, D. A., Bonk, C. J., Rodgers, M. L., Tikoo, M., & Powell, D. V. (2012). Instructor-made videos as a learner scaffolding tool. *Journal of Online Learning and Teaching, 8*(4). Retrieved from http://jolt.merlot.org/vol8no4/pan_1212.htm

Petress, K. (2008) What is meant by active learning? *Education, 128,* 566-569.

Prince, M. (2004). Does active learning work? A review of the research. *Journal of Engineering Education, 93*(3), 223-231.

Shackelford, J. L., & Maxwell, M. (2012). Contribution of learner-instructor interaction to sense of community in graduate online education. *Journal of Online Learning and Teaching, 8*(4). Retrieved from http://jolt.merlot.org/vol8no4/shackelford_1212.htm

Svinicki, M. D., & McKeachie, W. J. (2011). *McKeachie's teaching tips: Strategies, research, and theory for college and university teachers* (13th ed.). Belmont, CA: Wadsworth.

Thweatt, K. S., & McCroskey, J. C. (1996). Teacher nonimmediacy and misbehavior: Unintentional negative communication. *Communication Research Reports, 13*(2), 198-204.

Woods, R., & Ebersole, S. (2002). Becoming a communal architect in the online classroom: Integrating cognitive and affective learning for maximum effect in web-based learning. *Online Journal of Distance Learning Administration, 6*(1). Retrieved from http://www.westga.edu/~distance/ojdla/spring61/woods61.htm

Yazedjian, A., & Kolkhorst, B. (2007). Implementing small group activities in large lecture classes. *College Teaching, 55*(4), 164-169.

Chapter 9
Assessment of Classroom Learning

Wendy G. Troxel

A classroom is a curious environment. Whether in-person or online, it comprises a group of people exploring the known and the unknown, regardless of discipline and form of cognitive or creative expression. The goal is incremental improvement of skills, abilities, and/or dispositions that are observable in some form. Effective teaching assumes a dynamic and continual link between instructional strategies and learning and developmental outcomes. Angelo (1991) stated "the purpose of classroom assessment is to provide faculty and students with information and insights needed to improve teaching effectiveness and learning quality" (p. 17). In fact, McMillan (2013) noted, "Classroom assessment (CA) is the most powerful type of measurement in education that influences student learning" (p. xxiii).

Effective assessment in the classroom (a) requires multiple types of feedback collected throughout the semester; (b) connects specifically and intentionally to goals and learning objectives; (c) involves students in the process; and (d) ultimately results in clear evidence for summative judgment of knowledge, skills, and abilities (Bain, 2004; Shermis & DiVesta, 2011). Though faculty gain much insight through these assessments, students benefit most from the process and the results. Further, when students are involved in the development of measures and rubrics, scoring, and interpreting results, it gives them the ability to assess their own learning and progress, develop clear expectations of the performance expected, and evaluate their own efforts in relation to these expectations (Huba & Freed, 2000). In addition, some assessments have a critical development component that does not directly lead to summative judgments, such as grading. Rather, these assessments are part of the dynamic process of learning that helps promote academic and dispositional growth for both faculty and students.

Learning and Developmental Outcomes

Learning comes in many forms. Decades ago, Bloom (1956) and others divided the domains of learning into three areas: (a) cognitive (academic learning), (b) affective (value development), and (c) psychomotor (physical skill development). While there have been many variations on the themes since then, these three areas can form the basis of well-articulated learning and developmental outcomes, which can make goals explicit and are designed to elicit an action by the student to demonstrate knowledge, skills, and/or dispositions. They should be *clear, specific,* and *measurable* and connect directly to the teaching strategies. In addition, they should lead directly to appropriate and relevant assessment techniques to gather evidence of learning and provide feedback and judgment to students about their work.

Beyond a simple listing of course topics and general goals, every syllabus should articulate intended outcomes statements that describe the skills, abilities, and dispositions to be demonstrated (Grunert O'Brien, Millis, & Cohen, 2008). The examples below are structured and worded with an eye toward the selection of techniques appropriate to assess the learning and developmental outcomes.

- Students will effectively use language and nonverbal techniques, including voice.
- Students will compute various inferential statistics (e.g., *t*-score, Z-score, correlation coefficient) using both hand calculation and computer methods.
- Students will be able to analyze, interpret, and evaluate samples of good literature from each period (from Puritan to Postmodern), identifying and explaining an author's use of rhetorical strategies and techniques.
- Students will create and propose an on-campus civically engaged project to address a social issue or need.
- Students will be able to describe different types of of religious experiences, beliefs, and practices.

Once the elements of intended outcomes are understood, the focus of the statements is then on actions and evidence, which should be analyzed to examine the gap between intended and actual learning. In the future, the intended learning outcomes may need to be reviewed for appropriateness and clarity and revised accordingly. Different or modified instructional strategies (e.g., activities, resource materials) may be needed. Finally, assessment activities and products (e.g., formative and summative approaches to assignments, outcome expectations according to curricular alignment) may need to be revised in light of changes to learning outcomes and instructional strategies.

Formative and Summative Assessment

Assessments are often described as either formative or summative. *Formative assessments* are conducted during the instructional experience for the purpose of providing feedback and making improvement (Heritage, 2010). Classroom assessment techniques can be described as formative assessment in that the results are meant to inform both the teacher and the student of learning progress. *Summative assessments* are typically conducted at the end of a unit within a course or at the end of the course itself (Banta, 2002). Evidence from summative assessments is used to identify levels of attainment, make determinations about the students' achievement of expected outcomes, and compare results against an expected level (criterion) or benchmark (peer or baseline).

Direct and Indirect Measures

Assessment data are often described as either direct or indirect (Suskie, 2009). *Direct measures* require actual performance or demonstration by students to indicate how well they have attained the intended outcomes. Often, engaged learning is observable; the gap between intended and actual outcomes can be easily detected by both the instructor and the student and can be documented. The most common direct assessment (evaluation) methods are quizzes and tests, either locally developed or standardized tests appropriate to the discipline. Careful attention needs to be paid to validating exams for their intended purpose, which means ensuring adequate face and construct validity; predictive validity, if appropriate; reliability; and lack of significant bias.

There are many other options for actively capturing learning and development while it is happening, such as the minute paper—one of the most widely used classroom assessment techniques. This activity involves two simple, but critical, questions asked of students at any point in the semester: (a) What is the most important thing you have learned today (or this week)? and (b) What is still unclear?

These two questions reveal not only the important concepts that have been captured (i.e., assessment *of* learning) but also, perhaps even more importantly, require students to articulate what they do not yet understand (i.e., assessment *for* learning). The results inform the instructor of areas that may need further clarification and practice. They also engage students more deeply with their own learning styles and abilities. If the technique is used frequently, students get into the habit of paying closer attention during class or while studying and are better able to identify key concepts and areas where they still have trouble grasping the material (Chizmar & Ostrosky, 1998). As a result, they become more actively engaged with the course content.

The minute paper can be completed as a written in-class assignment, as an electronic survey in an online environment, or even on a smartphone using an application designed to take a quick poll of the level of understanding of a concept (Rosenberger, 2013). The responses are collected and reviewed, and the instructor addresses the results as soon as possible. The conversation is an effective one. Important concepts are reinforced with positive feedback, especially if the majority of the class indicated understanding, and students who are having difficulty are immediately alerted. If a large number of students indicated confusion on a concept, it can be attended to before moving on. This represents a critical moment in the pedagogical sequence within a unit or course. While there will always be differing levels of ability and preparedness, effective teachers know early and often when students are not "getting it" and adjust accordingly toward the mutual goal of academic success.

Indirect measures use evidence suggesting that learning has occurred without an actual demonstration (i.e., perceptions and reflections of learning). Accrediting agencies and the public are increasingly insisting on direct evidence of student learning, but information collected through indirect measures continues to be important. Examples of indirect measures are individual reflections on learning gains, satisfaction surveys, peer reviews, and exit interviews.

More Classroom Assessment Techniques in Action

Formative assessment techniques provide a mechanism to document deep learning and development as it happens (e.g., Angelo & Cross, 1993; Suskie, 2009; Walvoord & Anderson, 1998; Wiggins, 1998). These relatively simple techniques should not be casually constructed, however. Research on cognition and social-cultural aspects of education still reveals there is much to be learned about the effects of such things as motivation, self-regulation, and self-efficacy (among others) on learning (Brookhart, 2013; Kingston & Nash, 2011).

What follows are some examples of classroom assessment techniques that could be used throughout a course to gather feedback from students on the kinds of approaches described in this book. While it may be easy to choose a technique and find an application for it in the classroom, it would be more appropriate to address the conceptual aspect or approach first and determine what type of evidence will be useful to assess learning and development. For example,

- *Strengths-based approaches* to learning acknowledge and celebrate what students bring to the table. Goal-setting exercises ensure that instructor and students have articulated clear expectations for any number of topics (e.g., clarity of course content, personal and academic goals, group work, study habits, plans of study). When individuals rank their goals and match them with others, a rich conversation can take place. "Faculty can use the information this technique provides to increase student motivation by helping students make connections between their personal goals and course goals, and—where appropriate—by incorporating student goals into the syllabus" (Angelo & Cross, 1993, p. 290).
  In addition, effective instructors make an attempt to find out what students already know about the subject of the course. *Pretesting* is a term that often denotes formal cause-and-effect studies, but the concept is relevant to any learning environment. It is important to understand what students already know, can do, or value, in order to determine how the learning activities affected their knowledge, skills, and dispositions (Pellegrino, Chudowsky, & Glaser, 2001). The pretest can take any appropriate form (according to the discipline and type of subject matter) and be used with goal-setting exercises to involve the student within this very complex process. (See Chapter 6 on strength-based learning.)
- Group projects have been used with varying success in the classroom, but truly *collaborative* (or *cooperative*) *group learning* (i.e., *interactive group learning*) effectively uses the strengths and energies of peers on educational tasks. Two important elements of a successful interactive learning group are promotive interactions and group processing (Johnson & Johnson, 2009). Activities that involve verbal and written feedback to others regarding their contributions to the learning environment promote both

self- and collective efficacy, as well as accountability, and can "increase members' involvement in the group's efforts" (p. 369). (See Chapter 7 on interactive group learning.)

- Especially at the undergraduate level, class sessions are short, and it is difficult to get students up and running on course material for the day. The "RSQC2 (Recall, Summarize, Question, Connect, and Comment)" technique can be used to review previously covered material, work on transfer of knowledge, and get students intellectually engaged at the start of class (Angelo & Cross, 1993, p. 344). Students use the first few minutes of class to *recall* the most important concepts of the previous class, *summarize* the concepts in one sentence, construct a *question* still to be answered, *connect* the main concept or points to the topics within the entire course, and *comment* on their feelings about their own learning or the class to this point (Angelo & Cross, 1993). These one-page comments (or electronic survey) can be collected by the instructor or shared with fellow students. The RSQC2 technique might be especially usefully in the flipped classroom, providing a springboard for discussing and synthesizing content students are learning outside the classroom. Once learned, some students find it useful to start each class session with this technique on their own, even if it is not a formal process.
- Class discussions on sensitive issues are always a challenge. Important learning and development take place when controversial topics are discussed in an environment that encourages differences of opinion. However, those conversations can be difficult to facilitate if there is a sense that unpopular opinions will result in academic or personal retaliation. Students who fear they hold a minority view may choose not to voice their opinions even though it would be beneficial to the learning conversation to do so (Werder & Otis, 2010). There are a number of classroom polling techniques that can be used to capture real opinions in the room without revealing their source. Classroom clickers are used on many campuses to conduct quick polls, with the frequency of responses being posted on screen in real time. In a face-to-face environment, simple note cards can be used to record responses to prompts by the instructor (often in *A*, *B*, or *C* survey format). Students then get up and exchange notecards at least three times with three different people. Afterwards, individual students reveal the results of the card they are holding, having no idea who originated the response. This allows students "to discover

their own opinions about issues, to compare their opinions with those of their classmates, and to test their opinions against evidence and expert opinion" (Angelo & Cross, 1993, p. 258). There is historical evidence of the effectiveness of critical pedagogies in the development and maturity of students, as well as the activism that can result (Baker, 2011). (See Chapter 4 on critical pedagogy.)

- A technique called "double-entry journals" (Angelo & Cross, 1993, p. 263) collects multilevel feedback on selected reading assignments, including a column on the students' reactions to what they read and valued and one for their reflections on how they came to those values and opinions. Considerable attention and awareness should be paid, however, to the lens through which the instructor evaluates the responses (Kirkhart, 2005). This is a highly personal and vulnerable exercise that may reveal biases, untapped emotions, and even flagrant discriminatory beliefs. Care must be taken in the preparation and instructions for the activity, as well as to the response, to ensure an environment where reflection is safe and confidentiality is protected.

These and many other formative assessment techniques can capture knowledge, skills, and dispositions throughout a course or program of study. The series of activities and scaffolded assignments are intended to result in a comprehensive set of evidence. One tool, *portfolios*, can provide a systematic collection of learning gains.

Portfolios

Portfolio evaluation is designed to capture both direct and indirect learning and development. Campbell, Melenyzer, Nettles, and Wyman (2000) explained that portfolios are *not*

> a scrapbook of college course assignments and memorabilia … [but] an organized documentation of growth and achievement that provides tangible evidence of the attainment and professional knowledge, skills, and dispositions. Each portfolio is goal-driven, original, and reflective. (p. 13)

At the center of the definition is the contextual and authentic nature of the evaluation—it can be used to assess performance on real-world challenges and activities and provide the student tangible evidence of his or her own academic growth and abilities. It also offers faculty verification of the collective learning and achievement of students who have gone through a program of study.

Specifically, portfolios are collections of student work that exhibit to the faculty and student the progress made and achievements attained during a course, a sequence of courses within a major, or a program. These can be paper or electronic with a multitude of software packages available to support e-portfolios. They often include samples of student work, such as papers, exams, self-evaluations, course assignments or projects, videos, and other artifacts. Collecting student work over time provides a unique opportunity to assess a student's progression toward attainment of outcomes.

An added advantage of portfolios is that students are involved in the process of preparation and selection of the artifacts and examples to be included, resulting in reflective engagement (Fredrick, 2009). Rubrics are often applied to artifacts as well as complete portfolios to evaluate students' work for evidence of learning outcome attainment. A discussion of rubrics will be presented later in this chapter.

Portfolios provide an educational framework and physical mechanism for gathering and integrating learning and development and serve as a repository of evidence for multiple purposes and audiences. The process can be challenging, and a number of issues and questions must be addressed before launching a portfolio project, including,

- focus (audience and purpose),
- format (media),
- artifacts (pieces of evidence), and
- assessment and evaluation.

Focus (audience and purpose). When portfolios are used a number of questions surround their implementation. Is the portfolio electronic or paper? Who decides what goes into the portfolio—the student or the instructor? What pieces of evidence go into the portfolio? Who grades them, and is everything in the portfolio subject to grading? Who else has access to the items? Who owns the portfolio? The answers to these questions are framed by two foundational questions: (a) Who is the audience? and (b) What is the purpose?

The audience refers to anyone who has reason to look at and/or review the artifacts in the portfolio. It starts with the student. The most basic, informal portfolio is created every time a student organizes his or her work for a class into a notebook or electronic folder, and the work is collected primarily for the student's access. There is often little impetus for the student to go back through the work and reflect on it other than to review the contents to prepare for the final exam.

A second audience is the instructor, who reviews each piece of work the student submits and often provides feedback as well as evaluative markings before handing it back. As the course continues and based on subsequent assignments and activities, the instructor determines the student's level of competence according to the class requirements, and a final grade is earned for the course. In most cases, a faculty member does not review the earlier work again.

If the instructor chooses to have students build a portfolio in the class, there must be a well-articulated and intentional purpose for doing so. To determine which artifacts will be included in the portfolio, three purposes should be considered:

- **Showing mastery:** The products that are submitted to show mastery of a skill or content area will be contingent on the outcome statement for that particular course. For example, mastery of a writing skill in a first-year composition course will be at a lower level than the mastery expected in an upper-division creative writing course.
- **Demonstrating growth:** The instructor may want to capture evidence demonstrating the level to which the student has learned as a result of the educational experiences. To build the evidentiary record within the portfolio, there would need to be multiple pieces of work completed throughout the course.
- **Reflecting and synthesizing:** One of the most important aspects of learning is the student's awareness of his or her own growth and development (Pellegrino et al., 2001). A portfolio designed for this purpose would contain earlier work as well as the final product, and the instructor may add an activity asking the student to review the body of work and reflect on the evidence. Having the pieces of the learning puzzle together in one place and trying to describe the big picture often help the student synthesize the material in a deeper way than if the assignments and tests are isolated (Ambrose, Bridges, DiPietro, Lovett, & Norma, 2010).

The decisions to be made about the focus of the portfolio and inclusion of artifacts are dependent upon the intentions in each of these areas as well as the course learning and developmental outcomes. For course-based portfolios, the purpose is to show learning and development during that class (and according to the articulated outcomes), and the audience is the instructor and student. However, portfolios can also be used at the programmatic level to reveal student growth and the achievement of goals throughout a program, with a wider audience base that can include administrators and campus or community stakeholders.

Format (media). Paper portfolios have a long history in education and are most useful at the course level. They may simply be in the form of file folders or a binder with tabs; however, to save physical space or use during the job search process, paper portfolios can easily be converted to an electronic form (e.g., pdf documents; mp3, mpeg, or jpeg files).

Web-based or electronic portfolios are being used throughout education to provide the most dynamic platform for the gathering of evidence and assessment of individuals and cohorts. There are important considerations to be made regarding maintenance, cost, and ever-changing software and hardware capabilities. Some institutions choose to build their own systems—this provides the highest level of relevance and intentionality according to the intended outcomes of the programs but requires significant expertise in the area of computer programming and infrastructure management. Other institutions choose to purchase systems from outside vendors.

Artifacts (pieces of evidence). The portfolio provides the opportunity to contain both direct and indirect evidence of learning, which should come from the intended outcomes statements for the course. When considering the evidence to be housed in the portfolio, the issue of format is important but should not be the deciding factor. For example, if an intended outcome is to deliver a persuasive speech and demonstrate physical mannerisms that show confidence as a public speaker, a video clip of a speech may be a more representative piece of evidence than a written paper that would more conveniently fit in the student's binder. Further, the scope of the portfolio (e.g., number and type of artifacts, time period and context in which artifacts produced) should be determined. The selection of the artifacts to go into the portfolio may come from the student, the instructor, or both. Any number of pieces of evidence can be contained in a portfolio, such as

- papers and selected assignments,
- tests or exams,
- reflections and journal entries,
- peer reviews of selected works,
- video and audio clips of performances,
- photographs,
- assignment criteria (for context),

- art work,
- instructor feedback, and
- activity logs.

The range of possibilities is great; therefore, it is important the collection of evidence is gathered together in a systematic way and cross-referenced to enable interpretation and review of skills and abilities. Usually the student must provide a cover page written to describe the context for the evidence, as well as an indexing system explaining the content.

Assessment and evaluation. While the format of the portfolio is important in terms of access and structure, the more critical issue is how the evidence within the portfolio can be used for assessment purposes in the classroom. A number of assessment methods are discussed in the next sections.

Rubrics

Rubrics are scoring guides that define expectations for student learning in relation to specific outcomes (Quinlan, 2012). They describe what faculty look for when they evaluate a student assignment along with guidelines for assessing each of those aspects. Also called a *primary trait analysis* (Walvoord & Anderson, 1998), rubrics can be effective instructional tools for helping students understand faculty expectations and inspiring better performance by providing a mechanism to evaluate their own work before turning it in. Rubrics can enhance the feedback returned to students about their assignments, making scoring easier and faster, and typically reduce arguments about grading since expectations are clearly defined in advance. Following a rubric also leads to more accurate and consistent scoring across and between students (Lane, 2013).

A first step in the process is to identify the specific concepts and skills to be taught, and then designate assignments within the course that will produce evidence to assess the outcomes. For example, an intended outcome within an English course may address written communication and research techniques. A rubric to assess basic research skills in the final paper in the class might include the following elements (Figure 9.1):

- search criteria described (i.e., replicability),
- scholarly sources (e.g., relevant, current, varied),
- critical analysis (i.e., identification of arguments and gaps),

- conclusions (i.e., based on evidence presented),
- writing style (e.g., clarity, grammar), and
- format (e.g., sources cited in APA style).

Once the elements are selected, the next step is to determine the number and criteria of performance levels. While levels typically range from deficient to mastery, it is important to consider the implications of the terminology used to describe the level. The term *deficient* may appropriately indicate that a student has failed to include relevant materials within that element (e.g., a complete lack of sources cited in APA style), but in the learning environment, a new skill or ability should be acknowledged in a more positive and developmental way. For example, a range of descriptive levels might be *novice* or *beginning, developing, accomplished* or *proficient*, and *exemplary* or *mastery* (Figure 9.1). These levels may be assigned numerical values, which correspond to letter grades or points toward a summative total.

A simple method of writing descriptive criteria is to work from the edges of the rubric first. Most instructors can easily describe the elements of an excellent product or performance and a beginning or deficient one. Start with the word, *YES* or *NO*, and follow it with the description of the element to be observed. The middle columns represent a range of proficiency and can be prompted by *NO, BUT* and *YES, BUT* concepts (Figure 9.2). The *YES, NO*, and *BUT* operators can be eliminated or incorporated in the actual student feedback, and points could be assigned to allow for further delineation.

The development of the descriptors within each cell takes practice and continual review but, once established, can provide both the instructor and the student with a clear understanding of what is expected on that assignment (Quinlan, 2012). Students can use the rubric in the earliest stages of the academic product (or creative performance) or conduct a self-assessment prior to turning it in. The use of a well-designed rubric can also be effective when asking a peer to review a rough draft. This provides an additional opportunity for deeper engagement with the material and for collaborative learning.

Other Assessment Methods

Pretest and posttest evaluation is a method using tests (usually locally developed) administered to students at the beginning and the end of courses or academic programs (Allen, 2004). These test results enable faculty to evaluate students' growth and development in relation to the intended outcomes. This method can

Criteria	Beginning	Developing	Proficient	Mastery
Search criteria described (i.e., replicability)				
Scholarly sources (e.g., relevant, current, varied)				
Critical analysis (i.e., identification of arguments and gaps)				
Conclusions and recommendations				
Writing style (e.g., clarity, grammar)				
Format (e.g., sources cited in APA style)				

Figure 9.1. Sample rubric with affirming performance levels assessing research skills.

Criteria	Beginning	Developing	Proficient	Mastery
Conclusions and recommendations (8 points)	*NO* Conclusions are not connected to the evidence; there are limited recommendations for future action; implications for further study are not presented (0-2 points)	*NO* Conclusions are not connected well to the evidence presented *BUT* There are limited recommendations for future action; implications for further study are minimally presented (3-4 points)	*YES* The conclusions clearly emerge from the evidence presented *BUT* Lack a degree of engagement that impacts validity and meaning; recommendations for future action and implications for further study are presented but lack depth (5-6 points)	*YES* The conclusions clearly emerge from the evidence presented, and are unambiguous, valid, and meaningful; recommendations for future action and implications for further study are well articulated (7-8 points)

Figure 9.2. Developing rubric criteria with *YES; NO; YES, BUT;* and *NO, BUT* arguments.

be particularly useful to identify opportunities to improve the scope of instruction. By controlling for entry-level abilities through the pretest, this strategy provides an estimate of value added during the period of instruction or enrollment.

Video and audiotape evaluations can be used as pretests and posttests or summative assessment of students' skills and knowledge. Programs that have a performance component, such as theatre, music, art, and communications, are likely to use this method.

When faculty review and rate student performances collectively using common rubrics, this becomes a powerful direct assessment tool for instructional and curricular improvement. Ultimately, the ratings determined through rubrics or other evaluative process (e.g., correct answers on multiple choice tests) are calculated into grades.

Grading. For the vast majority of educational institutions, students earn letter grades, which are reported from the classroom to the record keepers at the institution. Overlap exists between grading and assessment, and grades are indisputably important for many reasons; but they are only an indicator of academic success in a particular class. They are not evidence of specific elements of student learning and development. Grades reflect a translation of the extent to which a student has mastered the subject matter, according to the criteria established by the faculty member.

Instructors generally have strict autonomy within their classrooms to determine the criteria and requirements necessary to earn grades. The formula for the demonstration of skills, abilities, and dispositions will differ depending on the course and instructor (e.g., a 90 may earn an *A* in one class but a *B* in another); however, it is up to the faculty member to determine how evidence of learning translates into letter grades.

Conclusion

The critical elements of a solid assessment framework at the classroom and program levels include

- clearly articulated, measurable outcomes of student learning and/or development;
- instructional strategies designed to give students the opportunities to achieve the outcomes;
- systematic strategies for collecting and analyzing evidence of student learning and/or development (e.g., classroom assessment); and

- interpretation of the results and articulating the ways in which they are used to change instructional strategies the next time (Huba & Freed, 2000; Suskie, 2009).

Support for students and teachers should be focused first on the place where learning takes place—in the classroom (broadly defined). The best teachers are reflective practitioners or scholars who continually search for ways to influence learning and involve students in that process (Bain, 2004; Werder & Otis, 2010). If this was accomplished more successfully and consistently across the institution, learning and development would be clearly observable for all stakeholders, and program assessment would not be left solely to academic leaders and other decision makers. More comprehensive assessment efforts fail when external mandates and initiatives are viewed as sets of narrow and technical requirements that force instructors to find their own ways to comply with accountability pressures to "get it done and turn it in," then go back to the isolation of their classrooms. When this happens, courses remain as silos and never contribute to a coherent curriculum of connected learning experiences that is obvious to students and can be documented as intentional. The broader goal, after all, is to improve student learning.

Learning implies an iterative sequence of initial deficiencies—multiple failures which decrease over time and effort—and the eventual application of new levels of behaviors, skills, or knowledge that can be observed from the outside (by the teacher) and embraced on the inside (by the learner). Assessment done right aligns well with what is known about learning, but often institutional systems support instructional strategies that miss important pieces of the teaching-learning-assessment puzzle. Done well, classroom assessment takes into account the dynamic and recursive nature of learning (for both students and faculty), which then also meets this higher standard of scholarship through real engagement of the stakeholders who matter most—students and their teachers.

References

Allen, M. J. (2004). *Assessing academic programs in higher education.* Bolton, MA: Anker.

Ambrose, S. A., Bridges, M. W., DiPietro, M., Lovett, M. C., & Norman, M. K. (2010). *How learning works: Seven research-based principles for smart teaching.* San Francisco, CA: Jossey-Bass.

Angelo, T. A. (1991). Ten easy pieces: Assessing higher learning in four dimensions. *New Directions in Teaching and Learning, 46,* 17-31.

Angelo, T. A., & Cross, K. P. (1993). *Classroom assessment techniques: A handbook for college teachers* (2nd ed.). San Francisco, CA: Jossey-Bass.

Bain, K. (2004). *What the best college teachers do.* Cambridge, MA: Harvard University Press.

Baker, S. (2011). Pedagogies of protest: African American teachers and the history of the Civil Rights Movement, 1940-1963. *Teachers College Record, 113*(12), 2777-2803.

Banta, T. W. (2002). *Building a scholarship of assessment.* San Francisco, CA: Jossey-Bass.

Bloom, B. S. (1956). *Taxonomy of educational objectives: The classification of educational goals.* New York, NY: Longmans, Green.

Brookhart, S. (2013). Classroom assessment in the context of motivation theory and research. In J. H. McMillan (Ed.), *SAGE handbook of research on classroom assessment.* Los Angeles, CA: SAGE.

Campbell, D. M., Melenyzer, B. J., Nettles, D. H., & Wyman, R. M. (2000). *Portfolio and performance assessment in teacher education.* Boston, MA: Allyn and Bacon.

Chizmar, J. F., & Ostrosky, A. L. (1998). The one-minute paper: Some empirical findings. *Research in Economic Education, 29*(1), 1-8.

Fredrick, T. (2009). *Looking in the mirror: Helping adolescents talk more reflectively during portfolio presentations.* Boston, MA: Teachers College Press.

Grunert O'Brien, J., Millis, B. J., & Cohen, M. W. (2008). *The course syllabus: A learning-centered approach* (2nd ed.). San Francisco, CA: Jossey-Bass.

Heritage, M. (2010). *Formative assessment: Making it happen in the classroom.* Thousand Oaks, CA: Corwin.

Huba, M. E., & Freed, J. E. (2000). *Learner-centered assessment on college campuses: Shifting the focus from teaching to learning.* Boston, MA: Allyn & Bacon.

Johnson, D. W., & Johnson, R. T. (2009). An educational psychology success story: Social interdependence theory and cooperative learning. *Educational Researcher, 38*(5), 365-379.

Kingston, N., & Nash, B. (2011). Formative assessment: A meta-analysis and a call for research. *Educational Measurement: Issues and Practice, 30*(4), 28-37.

Kirkhart, K. E. (2005). Through a cultural lens: Reflections on validity and theory in evaluation. In S. Hood, R. Hopson, & H. Frierson (Eds.), *The role of culture and cultural context: A mandate for inclusion, the discovery of truth, and understanding in evaluative theory and practice* (pp. 21-39). Greenwich, CT: Information Age.

Lane, S. (2013). Performance assessment. In J. H. McMillan (Ed.), *SAGE handbook of research on classroom assessment.* Los Angeles, CA: SAGE.

McMillan, J. H. (Ed.) (2013). *SAGE handbook of research on classroom assessment.* Los Angeles, CA: SAGE.

Pellegrino, J. W., Chudowsky, N., & Glaser, R. (Eds.). (2001). *Knowing what students know: The science and design of educational assessment.* Washington, DC: National Academy Press.

Quinlan, A. M. (2012). *A complete guide to rubrics: Assessment made easy for teachers of K-college* (2nd ed.). Lanham, MD: Rowman & Littlefield.

Rosenberger, T. (2013, May 13). *New online program creates automatic classroom communication.* Retrieved from http://www.videtteonline.com/index.php/2013/05/02/new-online-program-creates-automatic-classroom-communication/

Shermis, M. D., & DiVesta, F. J. (2011). *Classroom assessment in action.* Lanham, MD: Rowman & Littlefield.

Suskie, L. (2009). *Assessing student learning: A common sense guide* (2nd ed). Bolton, MA: Anker.

Walvoord, B., & Anderson, V. J. (1998). *Effective grading: A tool for learning and assessment.* San Francisco, CA: Jossey-Bass.

Werder, C., & Otis, M. M. (2010). *Engaging student voices in the study of teaching and learning.* Sterling, VA: Stylus.

Wiggins, G. (1998). *Educative assessment: Designing assessments to inform and improve student performance.* San Francisco, CA: Jossey-Bass.

Chapter 10 Summary and Conclusion

Barbara F. Tobolowsky

I started the book by arguing that faculty are central players in many of the current issues confronting higher education. Those tensions involve concerns about student learning, the increasing diversity of institutions and students, and the emergence of online education in its constantly evolving forms that affects not only vehicles for learning but pedagogy as well. Although faculty are often blamed by the public for any failures in the academy, I believe most instructors are well-intentioned but overwhelmed by the many demands on their time. This prevents them from rethinking and retooling their courses, even if they want to do so. Since time is the enemy of re-envisioning a course, this book's goal was to offer a select number of theories that may be the most helpful for faculty teaching undergraduate students. I hope we have succeeded.

Each of these chapters offers faculty suggestions about how to translate the theory to practice. In this conclusion, I discuss some of the highlights from the previous chapters that provided introductions to research, theory, and practice related to pedagogy.

Overview of Effective Practices

There are many lessons to be learned from research, which was the focus of Chapter 2. This overview of research discussed multiple factors that lead to improved learning. Not surprising, several of the ideas included here are also goals of the theories selected for inclusion in the book, so you will see these ideas echoed in other chapters. In this summary, I list a few of those elements identified that increase learning.

- Environments for learning that recognize and value the students' diverse backgrounds, cultures, beliefs, and preparations are important. To create these, instructors need to take the time to learn about their students because that knowledge affects pedagogical decisions.
- People learn in different ways; therefore, it is important to use multiple instructional methods to address students' various learning preferences.
- Timely feedback is critical in instruction regardless of the vehicle for learning.
- Student-faculty interaction matters. Frequent and high-quality formal and informal student-faculty interaction has a positive effect on student learning.
- Active-learning techniques result in increased learning. Instructors that facilitate active learning use discussion, require written work, give timely feedback, and allow sufficient time on task.

Foundational Theories of Learning

Some of the earlier pedagogical theories did not focus on the elements mentioned above. However, it is clear that each theory built upon those that came before it. Chapter 3 described some of those early theories and demonstrated that evolution. Here are some general lessons from that chapter.

- Rote learning is not ideal in most classroom settings. Theories that focus on memorization or punishment, such as behaviorism and cognitivism, are less likely to promote active learning.
- Theories that engage student emotions and motivations, such as humanism and constructivism, are more likely to result in learning that lasts.

Specific Learning Theories

Chapters 4-8 introduced a range of theories that focus on student diversity and different learning environments. Below is a summary of some of the key concepts and their application from those chapters.

- ***Critical pedagogy.*** The umbrella term, critical pedagogy, covers a range of theories dedicated to social justice, including feminist pedagogy, critical race pedagogy, contemplative pedagogy, and queer pedagogy. (See Chapters 4 and 5.)
    - In critical pedagogical theory, the focus is on recognizing and valuing the diversity of all student groups and acknowledging and challenging the privilege of the dominant culture.
    - Classroom efforts that engage discussion and self-reflection and challenge societal myths assist student identity development and improve critical-thinking skills.
    - **Highlighted applications:** Opportunities for reflection are valuable when investigating issues related to critical pedagogy. Using assignments that involve creativity (e.g., poetry, film, photography) are powerful vehicles for this exploration. They help point out societal, racial, and economic inequities.
- ***Strength-based pedagogy.*** This approach is based on the premise that motivation is critical to student learning. If students approach an assignment from a place of confidence, they are better able to grow when confronted with new challenges. The result is deep learning rather than surface learning. Students' motivation is promoted if instructors build assignments that use the students' areas of strengths, talents, and skills. (See Chapter 6.)
    - Because teachers using this theoretical approach believe that all students can learn and their role is to "foster that potential" (p. 81), instructors must determine what those strengths are at the outset.
    - Instructors need to know their own strengths to help guide their personal practice. This can be achieved through reflective journaling.
    - **Highlighted applications:** Because a strengths-based classroom approach can be new to most students, it helps for faculty

to explain the philosophy in the first class. Letting students know that all successful people got there through trial, error, and—most of all—practice can frame exploration in a pos-itive way. In addition, it is important to provide students with the reasoning behind assignments because it helps motivate their efforts. Finally, group projects that capitalize on individual students' diverse skills and talents create environments where learning is enhanced.

- ***Interactive group learning.*** This approach (also known as collaborative and/or cooperative learning) uses small groups as a vehicle for learning. Teachers become facilitators of learning rather than experts. Chapter 7 focused on this topic, but it is discussed in other chapters as well.
  - This type of learning recognizes the social element to learning; therefore, faculty need to be intentional in the organization of the groups and the assignments to capitalize on this factor.
  - **Highlighted applications:** Problem-based learning is one type of integrative group learning technique. Students are given a complex problem that does not have a right answer, and they work as a group to come up with a solution. This can be done using fictional or real-life case studies. Other common practices are think-pair-share, jigsaw, and team-based learning.
- ***Online learning.*** Active-learning techniques are well suited for online environments, specifically because they are unfettered by the constraints of a classroom. Simulations, the use of media, and games lead to the active engagement of the learner. (See Chapter 8.)
  - The main criticism of online courses is there is little opportunity for student-faculty interaction, which research shows is critical for student success. However, if faculty are intentional about the design of the course, online education does not need to jeopardize these connections.
  - One way faculty can connect with students is by providing feedback, such as imbedding quizzes in online assignments or transmitting audio (and/or video) feedback on written assignments. Also, the use of chat rooms and discussion options helps connect the learner with the teachers as well as other learners.

- Blended classrooms use both online and classroom elements and may provide the best of both mediums. Further, flipped classes can be developed where the direct instruction occurs outside of class and class time is spent using team-based learning activities. (See Chapters 7 and 8.)
- **Highlighted applications:** Problem-based learning techniques or inquiry-based learning works well in an online environment because of the availability of web resources to address vexing problems. In addition, curation tools, such as Pinterest and Storify, are current options that provide a space for students to present a range of images and/or media around a topic.

Lessons From Assessment

Chapter 9 discussed a range of assessment strategies that can be applied to any classroom setting. A summary of some of the key points and their applications from that chapter follows:

- Assessments should be designed to address the learning outcomes of the course. Outcomes statements need to be clear, specific, and measurable.
- Formative and summative assessment plays a critical role in providing feedback to teachers and students about the quality of the learning.
- Sometimes measures are direct, which means that the learning can be demonstrated (e.g., performances, tests); but at other times, indirect measures can be used to assess if there is a reflection of learning (e.g., satisfaction surveys, peer reviews).
- **Highlighted applications:** Common assessments can be pretests and posttests after material is covered in a class. Techniques include the one-minute paper, which asks students to say what they learned and what questions still remain, and the use of a rubric by a peer or the instructor to identify the strengths and weaknesses in the work in regards to the accomplishment of the learning outcomes. Rubrics can be created for an individual assignment or a portfolio, which is a cumulative review of work for a class.

Conclusion

This summary highlights some of the main ideas conveyed in the book. Perhaps the most obvious is that there is no silver bullet—there is not one approach that will work for all students in all circumstances. That said, it is apparent from the chapters that active-learning methods lead to increases in learning. However, active learning may look different from classroom to classroom and between learning environments (i.e., face-to-face, online, or blended).

Because of the great diversity in our students and our institutions, one of the specific goals of this book was to address the needs of a diverse group of students. By discussing a variety of theories and research within these pages, the intent was to provide insights into how to improve instructional practice so that it better supports the learning of a changing student demographic.

Finally, whole libraries could be filled with books on each of these theories (and are), but the life of a faculty member (pre- and post-tenure) is a constant struggle for time to accomplish everything she or he needs to do. Too often, an instructor's desire to adopt new teaching approaches gets lost in that time crunch. Many of us tell ourselves that what we are doing in a course is "good enough "and move on to other more pressing concerns, only making changes when they are forced upon us. Understanding these pressures, the goal here was to condense the current research on teaching and learning and provide a range of pedagogical approaches based on theory to help you plan your courses.

It was a daunting task. My first conversations with the National Resource Center folks were about how we should approach this goal. We started with a range of questions that faculty confront regularly. I listed many of them in the introduction. Two critical ones were, How do faculty address the needs of a diverse group of students? and How do instructors actively engage students regardless of the vehicle used for learning? Both questions seemed particularly relevant for faculty today and became our guides as the volume took shape. We ended up with the book you have before you. We hope this "best of" approach to teaching methods gives you the tools you need to facilitate the learning of the students in your courses.

At the heart of all faculty members is a desire to help facilitate the learning of our students, and this book is intended to provide inspiration and information for you to do that. Further, the primary issues confronting higher education, which served as our guides, will most likely continue to affect colleges and universities in the future. For this reason, we hope that the information shared in the book proves helpful to you in the coming weeks, months, and years.

Index

NOTE: Page numbers with italicized *f* indicate figures.

G

H

K

L

M

N

U

V

W

Y

Z

About the Contributors

S. Raj Chaudhury is the associate director of the Biggio Center for Enhancement of Teaching and Learning at Auburn University since 2009. In this capacity, he coordinates the Center's programs for graduate students and leads the Office of Distance Learning and Testing Services. His research interests are in the design and development of advanced technologies and research-based pedagogies as applied to teaching and learning of sciences and mathematics, for which he has received funding from the NSF, NASA, and U.S. Department of Education. In 2003-04, Chaudhury was a scholar with the Carnegie Academy for the Scholarship of Teaching and Learning. He holds a PhD in physics from University of California, Los Angeles.

Amy Collier received her PhD in family studies from Texas Woman's University and is the director of digital learning initiatives for the Office of the Vice Provost for Online Learning at Stanford University. Overseeing a variety of curriculum development and teaching initiatives, she partners with faculty to create high-impact online learning experiences by designing online and blended courses. She also conducts research to inform effective online learning practices across the University. As a result, Collier is well known as a persuasive advocate and invaluable resource for evidence-based instructional improvement, strategy, and planning.

James E. Groccia was the founding director of the Biggio Center for the Enhancement of Teaching and Learning and is professor of higher education in the Department of Educational Foundations, Leadership and Technology at Auburn University. He is a former president of the Professional and Organizational Development Network in Higher Education (POD). Groccia has authored, co-authored, and/or co-edited nine books and two journals on teaching, learning, and higher education, including most recently: *The Handbook of College and University Teaching: A Global Perspective* (2012); *The First-Year Seminar: Designing Implementing* *and Assessing Courses to Support Student Learning and Success-Instructor Training and Development* (Vol. 2, 2012); *To Improve the Academy: Resources for Faculty, Instructional, and Organizational Development* (Vols. 29-32, 2011-2013); and *Evidence-Based Teaching* (NDTL, No. 128, 2011). In addition, he has authored/co-authored numerous book chapters and journal articles, presented at national and international conferences, conducted workshops worldwide, and served as an advisor and consultant to institutions nationally and abroad. In 2011, Groccia was a Fulbright Scholar at the University of Tartu in Estonia where he taught, wrote, and conducted faculty development workshops throughout the country.

Heather Hardin is an assistant professor of nursing at Auburn University Montgomery. She earned her PhD in adult education from Auburn University and holds an Online Instruction Certification through Auburn University Montgomery.

Emad A. Ismail is the coordinator of the midsemester formative assessment program at the Biggio Center for the Enhancement of Teaching and Learning at Auburn University. In addition, he is a PhD candidate in Auburn's administration of higher education program and holds a PhD in plant pathology from the University of Illinois. He is a Fellow of the Higher Education Academy (UK), and a certified peer consultant. His research interests are in the qualities of excellent teaching and active learning.

Vijay Kanagala is an assistant professor of educational leadership and student affairs in the Department of Leadership and Developmental Sciences at the University of Vermont. His research interests include college access, success and completion of low-income, first-generation college students, intersectionality of education and immigration, and the collegiate experiences of students of color, international and generation 1.5 students. He employs contemplative pedagogy and spirituality to address social justice issues. Kanagala earned a PhD in education-educational leadership from Iowa State University.

Jillian Kinzie is the associate director for the Center for Postsecondary Research and the National Survey of Student Engagement (NSSE) Institute at Indiana University in Bloomington. Kinzie earned her PhD from Indiana University in higher education with a minor in women's studies. Prior to this, she served on the faculty of Indiana University and coordinated the University's master's program in higher education and student affairs. She also worked as an administrator in academic and student affairs at Miami University and Case Western Reserve University. Her scholarly interests include the assessment of student engagement; how colleges use data to improve; and the impact of programs and practices designed to support student success, as well as first-year student development, teaching and learning in college, access and equity, and women in underrepresented fields. She has co-authored numerous publications, including *Continuity and Change in College Choice: National Policy, Institutional Practices and Student Decision Making; Student Success in College: Creating Conditions that Matter*; and *One Size Does Not Fit All: Traditional and Innovative Models of Student Affairs Practice*. She is on the editorial board of the *Journal of College Student Development* and is recipient of a Student Choice Award for Outstanding Faculty at Indiana University and in 2005 and 2011 and the Robert J. Menges Honored Presentation by the Professional Organizational Development (POD) Network.

Stacey C. Nickson is the director of K12 Initiatives at Auburn University. She previously was the assistant director of the University's Biggio Center for the Enhancement of Teaching and Learning where she developed the Center's Cultural Insight Program promoting global communication skill development. Nickson's publications reflect her research interests, which include international collaborations for the preparation of future academic professionals and the enhancement of secondary school programs and global communication. She was a Fulbright Specialist at the University of Cape Town during the summer of 2013, working in the Center for Teaching and Learning to identify and codevelop best practices models.

Nana Osei-Kofi is director of the Difference, Power, and Discrimination Program; and associate professor of Women, Gender, and Sexuality Studies at Oregon State University (OSU). Prior to her appointment at OSU, Osei-Kofi was associate professor and director of the Social Justice Studies Graduate Certificate Program in the School of Education at Iowa State University. Her scholarship focuses on critical and feminist social theories and pedagogies, the politics of American higher education, and visual cultural studies and arts-based inquiry. Journals in which her work has appeared include, *Discourse: Studies in the Cultural Politics of Education, Feminist Formations, The Review of Higher Education, Equity & Excellence in Education, Latino Studies,* and *The Review of Education, Pedagogy, and Cultural Studies.* Osei-Kofi holds an MA. in applied women's studies and PhD. in education from Claremont Graduate University.

Laura I. Rendón is a professor of higher education in the College of Education and Human Development at the University of Texas-San Antonio. She is also co-director of the Center for Research and Policy in Education. As a research specialist on college preparation, persistence and graduation of low-income, first-generation students, Rendón is recognized as a thought leader in the field of contemplative education. In 2013, the Texas Diversity Council recognized her Among the Most Powerful and Influential Women in Texas. Rendón is credited with developing the theory of validation, which colleges and researchers have employed as a framework for working with and affirming low-income students. She also developed a pedagogic framework called sentipensante (sensing/thinking) pedagogy designed to help faculty employ contemplative pedagogic strategies that emphasize holistic student development and gear students toward goals such as social activism, service to others, and personal and social responsibility. Rendón earned a PhD in higher education administration from the University of Michigan, Ann Arbor. She holds an MA in counseling and guidance and psychology from Texas A&M University-Kingsville. She is author of *Sentipensante (Sensing/Thinking) Pedagogy: Educating for Wholeness, Social Justice and Liberation* and co-editor of numerous books and monographs, including *Transforming the First Year of College for Students of Color, Educating a New Majority, Introduction to American Higher Education,* and *Racial and Ethnic Diversity in Higher Education ASHE Reader.*

Laurie A. Schreiner is professor and chair of the doctoral programs in higher education at Azusa Pacific University. She has taught for 30 years, after receiving her PhD in community psychology from the University of Tennessee. She is co-author of the Student Satisfaction Inventory and has co-authored such books as *StrengthsQuest: Discover and Develop Your Strengths in College and Beyond* (2006) and *Helping Sophomores Succeed* (2010), *Thriving in Transitions: A Research-Based Approach to Student Success* (co-edited, 2012), along with numerous journal articles, including a three-part series on college student thriving for *About Campus* (2010). She is co-editor of the peer-reviewed research journal *Christian Higher Education* and has served on the advisory board of the National Resource Center for The First-Year Experience and Students in Transition and the editorial board for the *Journal of The First-Year Experience & Students in Transition.* Author of the *Thriving QuotientTM,* she maintains an active research program on college student thriving.

Barbara F. Tobolowsky is an assistant professor in the Educational Leadership and Policy Studies Department at the University of Texas at Arlington. Prior to this, she was the associate director of the National Resource Center for The First-Year Experience and Students in Transition where she oversaw the Center's publications, research, and conferences. Tobolowsky earned her PhD from the University of California, Los Angeles, in higher education and organizational change. Her primary scholarly interests include the academic journeys of students in transition (e.g., transfer students, sophomores) and media's role in influencing students' college aspirations and expectations as well as the public's view of academia. She has published numerous articles on these topics and co-edited the book, *Helping Sophomores Succeed: Understanding and Improving the Second-Year Experience* with Stuart Hunter and John Gardner. She serves on the advisory board of the Institute for the Study of Transfer Students as well as the editorial board of ASHE Higher Education Report monograph series and the National Resource Center's *Journal of The First-Year Experience & Students in Transition.*

Wendy G. Troxel is an associate professor in the Department of Educational Administration and Foundations at Illinois State University, where she teaches courses in quantitative and qualitative methodologies and program evaluation and assessment, works with students in the College Student Personnel Administration program, and advises doctoral students. Her research interests are in the area of teaching, learning, and advising in the first year of college; the impact of formative assessment techniques in the classroom; and the identification of teaching skills in precollege students. She previously served as the director of the University Assessment Office at Illinois State University. Troxel earned her doctorate in educational leadership at the University of Alabama at Birmingham (UAB), with special emphases in both educational research and education law. She also served as director of Undergraduate Admissions at UAB. She serves on the editorial board of *Planning and Changing Journal,* is on the review board of two professional journals (*NACADA Journal* and *Research & Practice in Assessment*), and is a member of the Board of Directors for The Hoenny Center for Research and Development in Teaching. Troxel is the current chair of the Research Committee for NACADA, the international organization of academic advisors.

Chenzi Wang completed her PhD in the administration of higher education at Auburn University in 2013. She was the graduate student coordinator for the Preparing Future Faculty (PFF) program at Auburn University's Biggio Center for Enhancement of Teaching and Learning and as has worked in the field of institutional assessment and evaluation since 2010.